BRAVE NEW WORLD

Other Titles in the Greenhaven Press Literary Companion Series:

American Authors

Maya Angelou
Stephen Crane
Emily Dickinson
William Faulkner
F. Scott Fitzgerald
Robert Frost
Nathaniel Hawthorne
Ernest Hemingway
Herman Melville
Arthur Miller
Eugene O'Neill
Edgar Allan Poe
John Steinbeck
Mark Twain
Walt Whitman
Thornton Wilder

American Literature

The Adventures of
  Huckleberry Finn
The Adventures of Tom
  Sawyer
The Call of the Wild
The Catcher in the Rye
The Crucible
Death of a Salesman
The Glass Menagerie
The Grapes of Wrath
The Great Gatsby
Of Mice and Men
The Old Man and the Sea
The Pearl
The Scarlet Letter
A Separate Peace

British Authors

Jane Austen
Joseph Conrad
Charles Dickens

British Literature

Animal Farm
Beowulf
The Canterbury Tales
Great Expectations
Hamlet
Heart of Darkness
Julius Caesar
Lord of the Flies
Macbeth
Pride and Prejudice
Romeo and Juliet
Shakespeare: The Comedies
Shakespeare: The Histories
Shakespeare: The Sonnets
Shakespeare: The Tragedies
A Tale of Two Cities
Wuthering Heights

World Authors

Fyodor Dostoyevsky
Homer
Sophocles

World Literature

All Quiet on the Western
  Front
Antigone
The Diary of a Young Girl
A Doll's House

THE GREENHAVEN PRESS
Literary Companion
TO BRITISH LITERATURE

READINGS ON

BRAVE NEW WORLD

Katie de Koster, *Book Editor*

David L. Bender, *Publisher*
Bruno Leone, *Executive Editor*
Bonnie Szumski, *Series Editor*

Greenhaven Press, Inc., San Diego, CA

Every effort has been made to trace the owners of copyrighted material. The articles in this volume may have been edited for content, length, and/or reading level. The titles have been changed to enhance the editorial purpose. Those interested in locating the original source will find the complete citation on the first page of each article.

Library of Congress Cataloging-in-Publication Data

Readings on Brave new world / Katie de Koster, book editor.
        p.   cm. — (Greenhaven Press literary companion to British literature)
    Includes bibliographical references and index.
    ISBN 1-56510-834-5 (pbk. : alk. paper). —
ISBN 1-56510-835-3 (lib. : alk. paper)
    1. Huxley, Aldous, 1894–1963. Brave new world.
2. Science fiction, English—History and criticism.
3. Dystopias in literature. I. De Koster, Katie, 1948–
II. Series.
PR6015.U9B677   1999
823'.912—dc21   98-48266
                                                              CIP

Cover photo: Brown Brothers

Copyright ©1999 by Greenhaven Press, Inc.
PO Box 289009
San Diego, CA 92198-9009
Printed in the U.S.A.

" *I think that fiction and, as I say, history and biography are* immensely *important . . . as vehicles for the expression of general philosophic ideas, religious ideas, social ideas. My goodness, Dostoevski is six times as profound as Kierkegaard, because he writes* fiction. **"**

Aldous Huxley,
Writers at Work

CONTENTS

Chapter 1: The Philosophy of *Brave New World*

Chapter 2: *Brave New World* as Prophesy

FOREWORD

*"'Tis the good reader that
makes the good book."*

Ralph Waldo Emerson

The story's bare facts are simple: The captain, an old and scarred seafarer, walks with a peg leg made of whale ivory. He relentlessly drives his crew to hunt the world's oceans for the great white whale that crippled him. After a long search, the ship encounters the whale and a fierce battle ensues. Finally the captain drives his harpoon into the whale, but the harpoon line catches the captain about the neck and drags him to his death.

A simple story, a straightforward plot—yet, since the 1851 publication of Herman Melville's *Moby-Dick*, readers and critics have found many meanings in the struggle between Captain Ahab and the whale. To some, the novel is a cautionary tale that depicts how Ahab's obsession with revenge leads to his insanity and death. Others believe that the whale represents the unknowable secrets of the universe and that Ahab is a tragic hero who dares to challenge fate by attempting to discover this knowledge. Perhaps Melville intended Ahab as a criticism of Americans' tendency to become involved in well-intentioned but irrational causes. Or did Melville model Ahab after himself, letting his fictional character express his anger at what he perceived as a cruel and distant god?

Although literary critics disagree over the meaning of *Moby-Dick*, readers do not need to choose one particular interpretation in order to gain an understanding of Melville's novel. Instead, by examining various analyses, they can gain numerous insights into the issues that lie under the surface of the basic plot. Studying the writings of literary critics can also aid readers in making their own assessments of *Moby-Dick* and other literary works and in developing analytical thinking skills.

The Greenhaven Literary Companion Series was created with these goals in mind. Designed for young adults, this unique anthology series provides an engaging and comprehensive introduction to literary analysis and criticism. The essays included in the Literary Companion Series are chosen for their accessibility to a young adult audience and are expertly edited in consideration of both the reading and comprehension levels of this audience. In addition, each essay is introduced by a concise summation that presents the contributing writer's main themes and insights. Every anthology in the Literary Companion Series contains a varied selection of critical essays that cover a wide time span and express diverse views. Wherever possible, primary sources are represented through excerpts from authors' notebooks, letters, and journals and through contemporary criticism.

Each title in the Literary Companion Series pays careful consideration to the historical context of the particular author or literary work. In-depth biographies and detailed chronologies reveal important aspects of authors' lives and emphasize the historical events and social milieu that influenced their writings. To facilitate further research, every anthology includes primary and secondary source bibliographies of articles and/or books selected for their suitability for young adults. These engaging features make the Greenhaven Literary Companion series ideal for introducing students to literary analysis in the classroom or as a library resource for young adults researching the world's great authors and literature.

Exceptional in its focus on young adults, the Greenhaven Literary Companion Series strives to present literary criticism in a compelling and accessible format. Every title in the series is intended to spark readers' interest in leading American and world authors, to help them broaden their understanding of literature, and to encourage them to formulate their own analyses of the literary works that they read. It is the editors' hope that young adult readers will find these anthologies to be true companions in their study of literature.

INTRODUCTION

One of the problems that engaged Aldous Huxley throughout his life was that of overpopulation. He wrote, lectured, and collaborated on film projects to try to move the world to deal with the issue. In his view, the issue was not simply over-population, but that inferior people were overpopulating.

Another of his interests, intertwined with the first, was the idea of eugenics—using deliberate breeding to increase desired inheritable traits, such as intelligence. This interest in eugenics was hardly surprising in the grandson of a man known as "Darwin's bulldog," Thomas Henry Huxley. T.H. Huxley had been one of the foremost defenders of Charles Darwin's theories of evolution, and eugenics seemed a natural extension of those theories. Before Darwin, the prevailing belief was that people were created exactly as they appear today, in God's image; therefore, it was sacrilege to think of their changing or being "improved." Once the idea took hold that mankind had evolved, like other species, scientists began trying to figure out how to guide that evolution.

Aldous Huxley, like his brother Julian, was a member of the British Eugenics Society (which claims, in an entry giving his membership information, that *Brave New World* is "a book about the Eugenics Society"). He wrote many articles on eugenics and evolution over a forty-year period, and *Brave New World* was conceived, at least in part, as "a little fun pulling the leg of H.G. Wells" over his rosy views on the effects of applied science and eugenics. (Wells was a friend of the Huxleys; not just a science fiction writer, he had collaborated with Aldous's older brother Julian on an encyclopedic work on biology, *Science of Life.*)

It only took Aldous Huxley four months to write *Brave New World,* but the idea of countering Wells's optimistic views had been brewing for some time. In 1927, five years before *Brave New World,* he had written in "A Note on Eugenics":

> It is obvious that all the superior individuals of the eugenic states will not be permitted to make full use of their powers, for the good reason that no society provides openings for more

11

than a limited number of superior people. No more than a few can govern, do scientific research, practise the arts . . . or lead their fellows. But if . . . every individual is capable of playing the superior part, who will consent to do the dirty work and obey? The inhabitants of one of Mr Wells's numerous Utopias solve the problem by ruling and being ruled, doing high-brow and low-brow work in turns. While Jones plays the piano, Smith spreads the manure. At the end of the shift, they change places; Jones trudges out to the dung-heap and Smith practises the A minor Etude of Chopin. An admirable state of affairs if it could be arranged. . . .

Personally, I find my faith too weak. . . . The intellectually gifted are notorious for the ruthless way in which they cultivate their gifts.

In *Brave New World,* Huxley postulated a different use of eugenics—one that to him seemed both much more likely and much more frightening in its rigid breeding of people to fit their positions like cogs in a machine. He hoped that by making it seem possible, he could encourage people to make sure his Brave New World never came to pass.

ALDOUS HUXLEY: A SELFLESS AND UNOBTRUSIVE HERO

Those who know Aldous Huxley only from the pages of *Brave New World* might be surprised to learn that the words used most often to describe him by those who knew him well were "kindness" and "gentle strength." Exquisite sensitivity and intense curiosity were combined in him with a rich intelligence, and all were nurtured in the fertile field of one of England's most prominent intellectual families. It was a stew that could easily have produced arrogance or impatience; instead emerged a man of quiet but profound passion for certain causes, yet serenity when facing personal crises.

HERITAGE OF THE MIND

Huxley's parents represented two strong, complementary strains of learned thought and thoughtful learning. His grandfather was Thomas Henry Huxley (1825–95), a prominent English biologist and writer. T.H. Huxley was one of the foremost supporters of the naturalist Charles Darwin, and fiercely advocated that all members of society should be taught the methods and ideals of the scientific method of research. T.H.'s son Leonard was an editor and publisher; he seems somewhat less prominent only because his father and two of his sons—Aldous and Julian—were among the most brilliant minds of their time.

Aldous's mother Julia was the granddaughter of Dr. Thomas Arnold, an English educator and historian who, as headmaster of Rugby, a British public school, had had far-reaching impact on education in England. Thomas Arnold's son Matthew, Julia's uncle, was a famed poet and literary critic. Julia's sister was Mrs. Humphry Ward, a successful and serious late Victorian novelist, and Julia herself founded a school for girls.

By the time Aldous Leonard Huxley was born, in the village of Godalming, Surrey, England, on July 26, 1894, Julia and Leonard Huxley already had two sons, Julian Sorrell and Noel

Trevenen (called Trev). Julian would follow in his grandfather's footsteps, becoming a well-known and widely respected biologist and writer. He remembered of his little brother,

> From early boyhood, I knew in some intuitive way that Aldous possessed some innate superiority and moved on a different level of being from us other children. This recognition dawned when Aldous was five and I a prep schoolboy of twelve: and it remained for the rest of his life.

> As a child, he spent a good deal of his time just sitting quietly, contemplating the strangeness of things. His godmother once saw him gazing out of the window, and asked what he was thinking about. He looked round, said the one word *Skin*, and turned his gaze out through the window again.

A SERIES OF CRISES

At the age of nine, in 1903, Aldous (who early dropped the "Leonard" from his name) was sent to a preparatory school, Hillside, as a boarder. His cousin Gervas Huxley reported that there were tears at being separated from his mother on the first day away, but they quickly gave way to the young schoolboy's intense curiosity, "the deeply interested curiosity with which, even at that age, he regarded the behaviour of the world and his fellows." His observation did not make him aloof, though; Gervas says "he was the most companionable of companions, and a full sharer in all our schoolboy nonsense, only with nonsense more imaginatively nonsensical than anyone else's."

The younger Huxley seemed to have an "inviolable inner fortress" to withdraw to when the miseries of school existence attacked, said his cousin, but his ability to put them into perspective was out of the ordinary, and he never gave way to violent emotion as the rest of his fellows did. Gervas marveled, "It was impossible to quarrel with him. Any waves of ill-natured spite or temper broke up at once when they met the shore of his integrity and complete unselfishness."

Aldous took part in school plays, playing Antonio in *The Merchant of Venice*, and Gervas remembered that "his performance as the unfortunate Merchant was of such pathos that parents in the audience were moved to tears." The two Huxleys and a third schoolmate, Lewis Gielgud (oldest brother of the actor Sir John Gielgud), also put out two issues of a literary magazine, which included Aldous's first appearances in print, a poem and a short story, which he illustrated himself. Aldous wasn't overly athletic, but on Sunday afternoons Gervas and Aldous, the "major and minor" Huxleys, would walk to Prior's Field, the school Aldous's mother had founded. Gervas remembered of his "Aunt Judy" that "initially I was somewhat in awe of her, but this soon vanished in the warmth of her understanding of young people and in her happy laughter. I soon realized why Aldous was so deeply devoted to her."

In 1908, Aldous entered Eton College, planning to study biology. Within weeks he was devastated to learn of the death of his mother from cancer. Years later, in his book *Eyeless in Gaza*, he gave expression to his sense of isolation and grief when he wrote about his character Anthony Beavis's bitter experience of facing his mother's death during his schooldays.

Less than two years later, an attack of *keratitis punctata*, an inflammation of the corneas, blinded Aldous in both eyes, forcing him to withdraw from Eton. Characteristically, he did not moan or complain; Gervas remembered finding him hunched under the covers in bed one very cold morning, from where he reported cheerfully, "You know, Gerry, there's one great advantage in Braille: you can read in bed without getting your hands cold!" He told another friend in delight that he could now read after lights-out. Gervas speculated that the months spent reading Braille, spelling out words letter by letter, may have lent clarity and economy to Aldous's later literary style.

His stoicism may have led to permanent injury, since the eye infection was ignored by the Eton authorities until it was well advanced. He didn't let blindness stop him from learning, though. Besides teaching himself Braille, he went to Marburg, Switzerland, to study music and improve his German language skills.

Although the vision in one eye was permanently damaged, after surgery Aldous eventually regained partial vision in the other. He had to give up his plan to become a physician—which his brother Julian judged a blessing in disguise, believing that Aldous was not suited to the day-to-day practice of medicine and that he would never have fully realized his genius if he had channeled it all into research. Nonetheless, his vision had improved enough that he was able to enter Balliol College at Oxford University in the fall of 1913 (the year Julian graduated with first-class honors in zoology). His room quickly became a favorite meeting place for his fellow students. Besides lively conversation, he entertained them with a new form of rag-time music, syncopated jazz, on the piano in the corner of the room.

He had less than a year of this charming environment before disaster struck again, to a brother who did not cope as well as he did with problems. Trev Huxley, born in 1889, was a bright student, a better athlete than his brothers Aldous and Julian, and better-looking than either of them. However, the pressures of living up to the examples set by his family proved too much for him. As Philip Thody explains,

> In 1914 the world seemed to lie at his feet. He nevertheless had an experience which, common though it may be for ordinary folk, is most unusual in Huxleys: he secured only second-class honours when he took Finals at Oxford. He also failed to secure a place in the Administrative Class of the Civil Service, and this inability to live up to the unremittingly high standards of the Huxley family, occurring at the same time as an unhappy love affair, proved too much for a personality whose inner conflicts were already expressing themselves in a nervous stammer. On 23 August 1914, Noel Trevenen Huxley hanged himself.

Aldous later wrote that it was "just the highest and best in Trev—his ideals—which have driven him to his death. . . . Trev was not strong, but he had the courage to face life with ideals—and his ideals were too much for him." The younger brother must also have wondered whether his own continued success in his studies despite years of blindness and limited vision had made Trev's "failure" harder for him to bear.

THE WAR YEARS

Trev had committed suicide less than three weeks after England declared war on Germany, entering what was to become World War I. When Aldous returned to Balliol that fall, many of his friends were off fighting, an impossibility for him because of his poor eyesight, which also kept him from filling many of the supportive roles civilians were needed for. Once again he was isolated at school, but during this period he met Lady Ottoline Morrell, who "presided over a casually assembled circle of the great and the promising at her manor house in Garsington, near Oxford," as Harold Watts describes it. With such guests as D.H. Lawrence, T.S. Eliot, Virginia Woolf, Bertrand Russell, Katherine Mansfield, and Lytton Strachey, the Garsington crowd was literate and educated, and determinedly free-thinking and free-speaking. Aldous fit right in. The relationship with Lawrence, in particular, would later become important for both men, and Huxley would edit Lawrence's letters when he died. In his introduction to that volume, Aldous recalled the first time he met the older author, in 1915:

> He was on the point, so he imagined, of setting off to Florida—
> to Florida, where he was going to plant that colony of escape,
> of which up to the last he never ceased to dream. . . . Before
> tea was over he asked me if I would join the party, and al-
> though I was an intellectually cautious young man, not at all
> inclined to enthusiasms, though Lawrence had startled and
> embarrassed me with sincerities of a kind to which my up-
> bringing had not accustomed me, I answered yes.

Although they did not see each other much for the next
eleven years, from 1926 until Lawrence's death in 1930 they
were frequently together and even more frequently in communication with each other.

In 1916 Aldous received first-class honors in English literature from Oxford and published his first book of poems, *The
Burning Wheel*. After graduation, he spent eight months living at Garsington, working on the farm and by those labors
feeling useful for the war effort. It was also here that he met
Maria Nys, a young Belgian refugee, and fell in love.

Juliette Baillot, who would later marry Julian Huxley, was
also at Garsington. As she remembered Maria:

> She was small, rather plump, but lovely beyond words, with
> large blue-green eyes matching an Egyptian scarab ring on
> her long finger, a delicate slightly aquiline profile and a small
> pointed chin under a full mouth. Her hair, cut short . . . , hung
> like a dark helmet. She had the vulnerable and defenceless
> look of a child with a mature body.

Although Maria returned his affections, the two could not
yet afford to marry. One biographer suggests that he could
have used some of the forty-thousand-pound estate his mother
had left, but his father had remarried, and the money was used
to educate his half-brothers. (The elder of his two half-brothers,
Andrew Fielding Huxley, was awarded the Nobel prize in
physiology in 1963.) There is no indication that Aldous felt any
bitterness, or dependence on anyone other than himself to
make a living, though. After a brief stint working as a clerk at
the Air Board, in late 1917 he took a job at his old school, Eton,
while continuing to write. Maria moved to London. After trying unsuccessfully to make a living teaching French, she
joined her mother and sisters in Italy.

ROMANTIC AND LITERARY SUCCESS

By 1919 Aldous had decided he was not cut out to be a
schoolteacher, and had instead found a job in what he called,
deprecatingly, "journalismus," joining the editorial staff of
the *Athenaeum*, writing reviews and articles and finding

enough financial stability to marry Maria on July 10. With the birth of their son, Matthew, on April 19 of the following year, he stepped up his journalistic efforts. He left the *Athenaeum* for a more lucrative position working for Condé Nast on the staff of *House and Garden* magazine, and accepted a position as drama critic for the *Westminster Gazette,* which entailed attending plays five times a week, an assignment he was delighted to quit once his novel *Crome Yellow* was published to great acclaim in 1921.

In 1923, his book publishers, Chatto and Windus, offered him the first in a series of three-year contracts to write two books of fiction, including one full-length novel, each year. With these contracts, he was free to live where he wished; he, Maria, and Matthew left England to live in Europe—primarily in France and Italy—for the next fourteen years, with time off for a round-the-world tour in 1925–26.

The years from 1923 to 1937 were full of travel, often in Europe, but also to Tunisia, Mexico, Bombay, and other exotic locales. The trip begun in September 1925, gathering material for the travel diary *Jesting Pilate,* took the Huxleys from Genoa, Italy, through India, Burma, Malaya, Singapore, and Japan, and brought them for the first time to the United States. After short stops in San Francisco, Los Angeles, Chicago, and New York, they returned to England, but were soon back in Italy.

In 1926, Aldous renewed his acquaintance with D.H. Lawrence, a close friendship between two seemingly unlike authors. Maria, who typed Aldous's manuscripts, also typed manuscripts for their friends. She was working on *Lady Chatterley's Lover* when Lawrence found himself embarrassed: she was using in conversation a four-letter word some people found shocking in the novel. Convinced he was the source of her vocabulary, he pleaded with her not to use the word, saying it would upset Aldous. She protested, "But Lawrence, you're always using it in *Lady Chatterley.* Besides, it is a very good word." He insisted that "it would shock Aldous." She knew her husband better than that, but agreed to watch her language—at least while Lawrence was around. Later, when the French police moved to outlaw the book and its author while Lawrence was very ill, Aldous and Maria called every influential member of the *literati* they could, asking them to intervene, and the police action was allowed to die . . . shortly before the author did. At Lawrence's request, the Huxleys joined him for what would be the last few days of his life, and were with him when he died, March 2, 1930.

Maria had brought a different sensibility than Aldous's to their marriage. Anita Loos, author of *Gentlemen Prefer Blondes,* became close friends with the couple in 1926, a relationship that became even closer when the Huxleys moved to the United States a decade later. Loos remembered Maria as

> unusual in her way as Aldous was in his. It was after I came to know her well that I learned the real meaning of the word "fey," for Maria supplied its definition; she lived a life of pure fantasy. She studied palmistry, believed in the stars, and even in the crystal-gazers of Hollywood Boulevard. At the same time, she had practical virtues that made her the truest help-meet I ever knew. As well as being Aldous's best loved companion, she was his housekeeper, secretary, typist, and drove his car in California. She protected him from the swarms of bores, pests, and ridiculous disciples who try to attach themselves to a great man, and all the while her unconventional reactions amused Aldous as well as amazed him.

She wasn't a sedate driver, either, when the Huxleys set out in fast cars to tour the countryside, wherever they happened to be. Aldous loved speed—he called it "the only *new* sensation this wretched century has produced"—and Maria obliged him, driving with precision and skill. She wasn't otherwise aggressive, though; she was a warm and generous hostess to their many friends. She and Aldous usually lived fairly simply, using their money to quietly help friends in need.

In 1931, Aldous's play *The World of Light: A Comedy in Three Acts,* had a short run at the Royalty Theatre in London. Aldous had long thought that plays were where the real money for writing could be found, an idea he would update when he moved to Los Angeles a few years later and began writing for Hollywood.

The year 1932 saw the publication of *Brave New World,* which described a world that rejected all that Aldous was— literate, artistic, intelligent, self-disciplined. He feared the world was heading toward realizing such a nightmarish reality, and felt that fiction was the best way to get his ideas across to the largest possible audience. More than sixty years later, readers still find echoes of their world resonating in the horribly cheery one he created in the novel.

Leonard Huxley, Aldous and Julian's father, died on May 3, 1933, a loss that did not seem to affect him nearly as deeply as the childhood losses of his mother and brother. Around 1935, Aldous became active in the pacifist movement, writing and lecturing in hopes of helping to prevent the devastation of another World War. Leonard Woolf remembered the "sweetness and fight" displayed by Huxley in an incident that took place sometime during these years:

> In the horrible years before the 1939 war when Hitler had begun the liquidation of the Jews, there were several cases of English men marrying German Jewish women solely in order to give them British citizenship and so saving them from being sent back to Germany. In one of these cases it became known that the Foreign Office was taking steps to prevent the marriage. Aldous and his brother Julian started a campaign against what seemed to be a barbarous abuse or misuse of authority and they mobilized all forces which might do something to prevent authority flinging the unfortunate victims to the Nazis. . . . Authority was beaten; the wedding took place; and all of us, including the bride and bridegroom, came to a curious, quiet, relieved wedding party in Albany. I cannot now remember the details of the case, but I know that the campaign was not an easy one. What I remember is that in action Aldous produced the same combination of strength and gentleness as he did in thought and argument. It was equally effective.

By 1937, after what was supposed to be a visit to the United States, the Huxleys decided to move permanently to California.

CALIFORNIA

By 1938, the Huxleys had settled in the Los Angeles area. The clear air and bright sunshine helped his vision, and the dry air of Southern California helped his lungs, which were never strong. (This was, of course, before smog became the hallmark of Los Angeles.) Once again Aldous was a member of a vibrant crowd, but this time the group's makeup was quite different from the intellectual elite who had gathered at Garsington. Here, a picnic might include Charlie Chaplin and Greta Garbo, Krishnamurti and other Theosophists from India, Bertrand Russell, Anita Loos, and the teenaged Matthew Huxley, Aldous and Maria's son.

The advent of the second World War was a rejection of the pacifism Huxley had been promoting for years; the subject was so grim that he seldom discussed it. However, it did affect his income, and he asked Anita Loos if she thought he might be able to get work writing for the movies. She quickly found a project for him and arranged an interview with the MGM producer. She reported that he and Maria called her shortly after the interview, disconsolate:

> "I'm sorry," Aldous said, "but I can't take the movie job."
>
> I wanted to know why not.
>
> "Because it pays twenty-five hundred dollars a week," he answered in deep distress. "I simply cannot accept all that

money to work in a pleasant studio while my family and friends are starving and being bombed in England."

"But Aldous," I asked, "why can't you accept that twenty-five hundred and send the larger part of it to England?"

There was a long silence at the other end of the line, and then Maria spoke up.

"Anita," she said, "what would we ever do without you?"

Unlike F. Scott Fitzgerald, who also tried writing for the movies but nearly came to blows over artistic differences, Huxley was successful in writing literate scripts that Hollywood could accept, or at least adapt. Oddly, much of his work seems to have been for movies about women: *Madame Curie* (his first try, the studio judged his treatment too scientific, and passed it along to others, including Fitzgerald, for more "fixing"), Jane Austen's *Pride and Prejudice*, Charlotte Brontë's *Jane Eyre.*

During this same period, he wrote *The Art of Seeing,* published in 1942. The book described the Bates method of exercises for strengthening the eyes and improving vision, a method he firmly believed in after having used it to help his failing eyesight. The Bates method provoked passionate response from both advocates and denigrators, and this book was wildly praised and soundly drubbed. It was far from the last time his ventures into science and medicine would prove controversial.

Over the remaining years of his life, Aldous would explore dianetics with L. Ron Hubbard, mysticism with various Eastern practitioners, psychedelics with Allen Ginsberg and Timothy Leary. After taking mescaline in 1953, he wrote *The Doors of Perception*—a title taken from a poem by William Blake, and adopted by Jim Morrison when he named his rock group The Doors. Huxley was always trying to push the boundaries of the mind, to see further and understand more. In the early days of enthusiasm for such drugs as mescaline, peyote, and LSD, when medical doctors were using them to explore both their effects on "normal" minds and what they might reveal about abnormal ones, such as those suffering from schizophrenia, he volunteered as a subject for experimentation. Dr. Humphry Osmond administered to him his first dose of mescaline; Huxley had prepared for the occasion by obtaining a dictaphone to record his impressions.

Huxley valued mind-altering drugs not for recreational use, but as a serious attempt to expand meditative and mystical states of mind—the ways native religions had originally used them. Biographers estimate that he used psychedelic drugs perhaps a dozen times; each time he carefully documented the experience, and shared his findings with others who were exploring their effects. However, the idea that a member of the intellectual elite would seriously explore the use of psychedelics was often abbreviated to an inference of general support for their recreational use by those who used such drugs for the thrill of the trip.

THE LAST YEARS

In March 1954, when Maria Huxley was diagnosed with cancer that she suspected would be terminal, she insisted that the doctor tell her the truth—and *not* tell Aldous: "You must tell *me*. You must *not* tell my husband. My husband has a book to finish and must have peace of mind." She continued to travel with him, to New York, to France, Egypt, Cyprus, Istanbul, Greece, Italy. In Rome, she visited a friend, a psychotherapist named Laura Archera, a woman she said was interested in "our kind of things"; when Laura visited, she and Maria would disappear for long talks together.

After the Huxleys returned to the United States, Maria's condition continued to deteriorate despite x-ray treatments and other, less orthodox methods. When she died on the morning of February 12, 1955, Aldous was with her, helping her through the experience, reminding her how much she was loved, telling her she could go forward into love.

Maria's death left Aldous feeling, he said, "as if I had been amputated." His friends and loved ones were delighted when he remarried in 1956, choosing his and Maria's friend Laura Archera as his second wife.

In 1958, he looked back at his most famous work, *Brave New World*, and compared it to the changes that had been made in the real world in the past quarter of a century. He wrote his observations in *Brave New World Revisited*, deciding that the world had progressed more quickly toward the horrors he had envisioned than he had conceived would be possible. He also noted that he would have given the Savage a third choice, a rational one, if he were writing the book then, with the benefit of his greater maturity and experience.

In 1959 he gave a series of lectures on "The Human Situation" as visiting professor at the University of California at Santa Barbara and was given the Award of Merit for the Novel from the American Academy of Arts and Letters. The following year he presented another prestigious lecture series,

"What a Piece of Work Is Man," as Centennial Carnegie Visiting Professor at the Massachusetts Institute of Technology.

When he was diagnosed as having cancer of the tongue in 1960, he refused the recommended surgery, which would have removed half his tongue and made it difficult for him to communicate verbally. He chose instead to be treated with radium needles, which did beat back the cancer for a while.

In 1961, Aldous and Laura Huxley's home was destroyed by fire; he lost his manuscripts, Maria's diaries, and everything else he owned. He told Dr. Osmond, "I took it as a sign that the grim reaper was having a good look at me," and explained to another friend, Robert Hutchins, "I am evidently intended to learn, a little in advance of the final denudation, that you can't take it with you." He accepted the loss with a certain serene humor, only remarking to one friend that he regretted not having earlier taken his advice about donating his manuscripts to a library.

Dr. Max Cutler, who treated him for his cancer, reported that Huxley "considered his own illness as a curious phenomenon which extended his own capacity for experience." After his tongue healed, it was scarcely a year and a half before Cutler found cancerous glands in Huxley's neck. As the disease progressed, the patient complained only about being too tired to do as much work as he wanted to do. He kept working, finishing his last essay, "Shakespeare and Religion," just a day or two before he died.

Timothy Leary visited his dying friend, and later remembered it this way:

> I spent the afternoon of Nov. 20, 1963, at Huxley's bedside, listening carefully as the dying philosopher spoke in a soft voice about many things.

> We fashioned a pleasant little literary fugue as he talked about three books he called "Parodies of Paradise," his own *Island,* Orwell's *1984* and Hesse's *Bead Game.*

> Aldous told me with a gentle chuckle that Big Brother, the beloved dictator of Orwell's nightmare society, was based on Winston Churchill. "Remember Big Brother's spell-binding rhetoric about the blood, sweat and fears requisitioned from everyone to defeat Eurasia? The hate-sessions? Priceless satire."

> As soon as he said this, I "got it." Sure, and the hero's name is Winston Smith.

> Aldous was, at that moment in time, fascinated by the Tibetan Book of the Dying, which I had just translated from Victorian English to American. This manuscript, which was later pub-

lished as *The Psychedelic Experience*, was used by Laura Huxley to guide Huxley's passing. . . .

Two days later Aldous Huxley died. His passing went almost unnoticed because John F. Kennedy also died on Nov. 22, 1963. It was a bad day for utopians and futurists all over.

AT HOME IN TWO CULTURES

David Cecil, in memorializing Huxley, wrote that he was that rare being at home in two cultures, the scientific and the literary, whose points of view so often seem mutually exclusive. His vision was not a comfortable one; in fact, it is often horrifying—but not hopeless. Cecil concludes:

> He had a profound sense of some spiritual reality, not to be apprehended by the senses, existing beyond the confines of time and space, serene, inviolate, ineffable. He was never able to pin down this awareness in a dogmatic formula: he did not attempt to chart the limits and extent of this spiritual region. . . . None the less, the spiritual world was intensely real to him, irradiating his soul with "bright shoots of everlastingness" and imbuing it with a fortitude that stood the shocks inflicted on him by fate. Aldous Huxley was threatened all his life with blindness, and in his last years he came to know that certain death was coming to him soon. Yet always he maintained his spirit unshaken. The distinguished artist, the bold thinker, was also a selfless and unobtrusive hero.

CHAPTER 1

The Philosophy of *Brave New World*

READINGS ON
BRAVE NEW WORLD

The Self Cannot Survive in Huxley's Utopia

Charles M. Holmes

Brave New World is more than a distressingly accurate picture of the results of uncontrolled technology, writes Charles M. Holmes. It is Huxley's exploration of the relationship between the self and contemporary culture, he declares, and it represents the author's fear that that culture endangers the survival of the individual self. Holmes is the author of *Aldous Huxley and the Way to Reality*, from which this essay is excerpted.

Though Huxley was before long to become a kind of mystic, he first became an even greater sceptic—in his next collection of essays[1] and in the best known of all of his novels. In "Beliefs and Actions" of *Music at Night* (1931) his scepticism is explicit. . . . His scepticism, rooted in his psychological bias, combined with decided opinions about the destiny of modern culture, became the bones and the heart of *Brave New World* (London: Chatto & Windus, 1932).

Not all of Huxley's rigid, spiritless, yet self-indulgent utopia is anticipated in the essays of *Music at Night*, but many principles are enunciated there. "If society continues to develop on its present lines," Huxley claims in one selection, "men will come to be valued more and more, not as individuals, but as personified social functions."[2] Hence the Alphas, Betas, and Epsilon-minus semi-morons, the Arch-Community Songster and the World Controllers. Another essay worries about Henry Ford's industrial religion. Anticipating the Savage in his debate with Mustapha Mond, Huxley finds no other creed demanding such cruel "mutilations of the human psyche"; it has no place "for artists, mys-

---

1. *Music at Night and Other Essays* (Garden City, N.Y.: Doubleday, Doran and Company, Inc., 1931). 2. "On the Charms of History and the Future of the Past," p. 131.

tics, or even, finally, [for] individuals."[3] The world of the novel features the "conscription of consumption"; even the games force citizens to consume. Under the unlikely title of "Selected Snobberies" the same economics, in embryo, appear in *Music at Night:* "Organized waste among consumers" is even today "the first condition of our industrial prosperity."[4] The very spirit of Huxley's sensate, Fordian culture is suggested in the selection "Foreheads Villainous Low": "The more noise you listen to, the more people you have round you, the faster you move and the more objects you possess, the happier you will be—the happier and also the more normal and virtuous."[5] Other details and motifs are anticipated also—the feelies, the emphasis on sex, even the presence of inner conflict in the man of unusual gifts. But the scepticism of *Music at Night* is the foundation of the novel. The writer of *Brave New World*, as Huxley later put it himself, was no life-worshipper but instead a "Pyrrhonic aesthete," too "amused" and detached to care that the world was going the way he showed.[6]

Brave New World also embodies a tendency even more entrenched than Huxley's scepticism. As Huxley recognized when he called himself a Pyrrhonist, the shape of the novel is partly dialectical.[7] It presents a successful, self-perpetuating culture in graphic, almost infinite detail, yet it also offers other choices than that culture, almost surreptitiously, and in a variety of ways.

The debate between Mustapha Mond and John the Savage is dialectic in cogent, obvious form. Disgusted by almost everything he has seen in Fordian culture and overwrought by his mother's death from soma, the Savage has caused a riot by heaving out the window boxes of pills. Then calmed by soma vapor and a "Synthetic Anti-Riot Speech," hustled with his compatriots into the office of Mustapha Mond, the Savage discusses with Mond the merits of civilization. Their first concern is happiness and its price. The Savage defends the beauty of *Othello*; Mustapha claims that high art must be sacrificed to maintain the stability on which happiness depends. The Savage notes the maggot-like ugliness of the Bokanovsky groups; the Controller, admitting his own dis-

---

3. "To the Puritan All Things Are Impure," pp. 159–160. 4. "Selected Snobberies," p. 199. 5. "Foreheads Villainous Low," pp. 185–186. 6. Foreword to *Brave New World*. Collected Edition (London: Chatto & Windus, 1950), p. viii. 7. *Pyrrhonism:* extreme or absolute scepticism; *dialectical:* relating to logical discussion or argumentation.

like, sees them as "the foundation on which everything else is built, . . . the gyroscope that stabilizes the rocket plane of state on its unswerving course." Helmholtz interjects the hypnopaedic claims for science; Mustapha sees pure science as "potentially subversive."[8] The new society has made its choice: happiness depends upon stability, and stability demands the stifling of every creative act, unless it will without question reinforce the state.

THE ENEMIES OF HAPPINESS

As the debate continues, the enemies of happiness change from art and science to religion. Rummaging in a safe stuffed with forbidden books, the Controller hauls out the Bible, *The Imitation of Christ, The Varieties of Religious Experience,* some Newman and some Maine de Biran. In Newman, identified as an "old Arch-Community Songster," Mustapha reads that our happiness is to view ourselves as the property of God. From Biran he quotes a passage on sickness and old age, and the consequent emergence of the religious sentiment and the consciousness of God. Biran's analysis is irrelevant: the religious sentiment is supposed to "compensate for our losses," but in the brave new world the losses no longer appear. When the Savage answers feebly that it's "natural" to believe in God, Mustapha counters by making fun of F.H. Bradley, who didn't realize that "one believes things because one has been conditioned to believe them." As the Savage articulates his presuppositions and ideals, Mustapha shows that none of them applies. At the end the two men agree to disagree. Mustapha's goal remains the childlike happiness of others while the Savage insists on freedom, on the right to be unhappy, even with the ugliness, fear, and pain which that right must entail.[9]

Mustapha's side of the dialectic begins much earlier, in chapter 3, in one element of a dizzy, accelerating montage. Addressing a touring group of "Hatchery and Conditioning" students, his slant this time is psychological. His target is the now mysterious institution of the family, with all the psychological overtones that that institution implies. Claiming Freud this time as his prophet instead of Ford, he pictures the "home" in lurid, exaggerated terms, as "stiflingly over-inhabited by a man, . . . a periodically teeming woman, . . . a

8. Chapter XVI. 9. Chapter XVII.

rabble of boys and girls of all ages." It is "as squalid psychically as physically," so "hot" is it with the frictions of life,
with the "suffocating . . . insane, obscene relationships between the members of the family group." Hence the need to
subdue and channel off emotion, "to make your lives," the
Controller tells his hearers, "emotionally easy—to preserve
you, so far as that is possible, from having any emotions at
all." Desires are relieved or satisfied as soon as they arise, by
entertainment, copulation, ritual and drugs. Stability is
again the "primal and ultimate need." And he races through
the establishment of the seventh-century A.F. world—
through the death of liberalism, "Simple Life," and culture;
through the development of ectogenesis, conditioning, and
hypnopaedia; through the destruction of historical monu-
ments, and the replacement of God by Community Sings and
Solidarity Services; through the discovery of soma—the perfect drug—and finally the hormonal conquest of old age.[10]

SHAKESPEAREAN VALUES

Mustapha's distorted comments, of course, are dialectically
countered by the words and the living example of the Savage, and not only in his idealistic statements during the
novel's final debate. Brought up in his New Mexican Reservation by a "civilized" mother abandoned among primitives,
the Savage represents in his grotesque suicide Huxley's "lunatic" alternative of "*Penitente* ferocity."[11] But he is a much
more ingenious and effective opponent of Mustapha by
virtue of his ready knowledge of Shakespeare's poems and
plays. Rejected by the natives because of his mother's
promiscuity, John has spent many an hour on a battered volume of Shakespeare's works. To comprehend the London he
has been thrust into he must employ Shakespearean, and
hence pre-Fordian, terms. Almost every cultural value represented in the plays has been discarded by the society in
which he suddenly appears. Whereas frustrated love leads
Helmholtz Watson to guffaw, John thinks of his beloved
Lenina as the "rich jewel in an Ethiop's ear" who cannot be

10. Sir Julian Huxley says that Aldous did not go to him for the "biological facts and
ideas" of the novel, but got them from his own reading and "occasional discussions
with me and a few other biologists, from which we profited as much as he." Julian
Huxley, ed., *Aldous Huxley: A Memorial Volume* (London: Chatto & Windus, 1965), p.
22. 11. The Huxley of 1946 has already published *The Perennial Philosophy* and suggests its ideas as a third alternative to the "insanity" of the super-civilized world and
the "lunacy" embodied in the primitive religion of the Savage's Indian village. Foreword to *Brave New World*, pp. vii–viii.

approached "before all sanctimonious ceremonies . . . with full and holy rite" have been performed. So imbued is he with Shakespearean morality, so ridden with guilt by any suggestion of lust, that when Lenina offers her charms he becomes the wrathful vindictive Othello, and eventually the aged Lear condemning lechery. Love, chastity, marriage and other Shakespearean socio-ethical concepts are, until John presents them, almost totally unknown. When Helmholtz hopes for creative self-fulfillment he nurtures a feeling he could not understand before his own reading of the plays. The moth-eaten volume and the priceless treasure it contains become the symbol of the values, all but forgotten, of our culture. Bernard Marx also rejects the sterile assumptions of his culture. He "doesn't like Obstacle Golf"; he even likes to be alone; and he joins in the soma battle with his anarchist friends. Obviously he too supports John's side of the dialectic.

THE WEAPON OF IRONY

But the most effective answer to Mustapha is . . . a persistent, even relentless ironic tone. The promises and values argued directly by Mustapha Mond are throughout the novel immersed in ironic dialogue. Every detail seems to embody its ironic opposite; its very appearance implies amusing and deprecating comment. When babies are manufactured on the Hatchery assembly line, we think of the mysteries of birth, now killed by the machine. "Community, Identity, Stability," the motto of the state, echoes the contrasting slogan of the eighteenth-century Jacobins. Institutional proper names immediately ridicule themselves: Human Element Manager and Assistant Fertilizer-General; the Hounslow Feely Studios, the Fordson Community Singery and the Young Women's Fordian Association; The Westminster Abbey Cabaret and Propaganda House; Electro-magnetic Golf, Centrifugal Bumble-puppy, and the Semi-Demi-Finals of the Women's Heavyweight Wrestling Championship. The characters' names are comically ironic: Benito Hoover, Polly Trotsky, Morgana Rothschild, Sarojini Engels. And so of course are the nursery rhymes: "Streptocock-G to Banbury-T/To see a fine Bathroom and W.C."

Against the mocking background of these cultural details, we watch the characters in their ironic choices and acts. No reader forgets the conditioning scene of chapter 3, where infants crawling toward flowers and books are greeted with electric shocks and clanging bells. When the men and their "pneumatic" women complete their daily routine, they play Riemann-surface tennis or indulge in unrestricted sex. Periodically pseudo-religious services are held: the communicants gather in a circle, pass around the soma-cup, sing Solidarity Hymns, listen to a piped-in, tremulous voice, and complete the ritual by copulating on the floor. The ironic knife cuts, of course, in both temporal directions. The proper names, the institutions, the cultural patterns are originally ours. During its composition, Huxley saw *Brave New World* as a "revolt" against "the horror of the Wellsian Utopia." [12] Yet he extrapolated his vision of the future from his sceptical, detached observations of the present. A projection of what our culture may become, the novel seems each day to comment more accurately on us now.

By now a classic, its title a household phrase, the novel does have significant defects. Bernard Marx is [an] ineffectual romantic idealist, . . . and hence [a] partial projection of Aldous Huxley himself. At first he is a useful, even sympathetic figure, sensitive to the beauties of the ocean and disturbed by the treatment of Lenina as "so much meat." But Huxley cannot be serious about his alienation. Having chosen to be the amused, Pyrrhonic aesthete, Huxley cannot simultaneously—in this novel, at least—identify with the unamused, self-conscious man, Bernard. With the help of shallow psychology he is turned into an insignificant fool, and eventually shoved almost entirely out of the way. Another weakness appears in the treatment of John the Savage, whose early years constitute an overwritten, unconvincing part of the novel.

THE RELATIONSHIP BETWEEN SELF AND CULTURE

Yet on the whole the Savage is one of Huxley's best creations, effective as a Shakespearean, as a debater, as an idealistic worshipper of Lenina. At the end he helps Huxley to shatter the novel's tone, and to assert dramatically one of its most important themes. John has been cursed with an id-and-superego split, a war between ideals and the sexuality those ideals repress. Stimulated by Lenina to both romantic love and physical lust, his response is to purge his guilt in grotesquely masochistic ways, by drinking mustard-water or

---

12. *Letters of Aldous Huxley*, ed. Grover Smith (London: Chatto & Windus, 1969), p. 348.

slashing himself with a whip. But Darwin Bonaparte's hidden cameras ruthlessly record his private life, and his activities become known throughout the Western world. When swarms of visitors, and Lenina, arrive where he has been living alone, the brave new world has trapped him once and for all. His superego collapses in an orgy, and the only thing left for him is self-destruction. Like Bernard and Helmholtz but far more helplessly, John has tried to find and live his selfhood. Selfhood, however, must be allowed and then nourished by culture. John's suicide, motivated by guilt, symbolizes the fact that in this world no true self can survive.

Hence *Brave New World* is more than another Huxley dialectic, and more than a damningly accurate vision of technological emptiness. It is an exploration in the most significant existentialist tradition of the relationship between the self and contemporary culture.[13] In *Do What You Will* Huxley had treated the self in almost total isolation and produced an oversimplified and impossible prescription. Now purged of his willed desire to "worship life," Huxley examines the problem in a fruitful though frightening way. Like Karl Jaspers' *Man in the Modern Age* published the year before, *Brave New World* asserts—though Huxley later would deny it—that the hopes of men are "no longer anchored in Transcendence."[14] Jaspers and Huxley both recognize the growing power of the state. Both are concerned about the authenticity of the self in what Jaspers calls an era of "advanced technique." Both show a kind of personal concern, Jaspers through his deeply serious, meditative tone, Huxley through Bernard, Helmholtz, the Savage, and at moments even Lenina and Mustapha Mond. But Jaspers stands beyond the incisive ironies of *Brave New World.* He believes that there "is no human existence without cleavage,"[15] yet that every man must "fight wittingly on behalf of his true essence";[16] and he is ready to comment on what mankind can become. Huxley, though he apparently still personifies the cleavage, will eventually believe that it can and must be healed. He will fight for his essence in his own unusual way, and offer his own far more elaborate views on the destiny that mankind, if it will decide to, can grasp.

13. William Spanos, to whom I am indebted for this idea, hints at the analogy between Mustapha Mond and the Grand Inquisitor, with *Brave New World* an existentialist retelling of Dostoyevsky's tale. *A Casebook on Existentialism* (New York: Thomas Y. Crowell Co., 1966), pp. 4, 13. 14. *Man in the Modern Age* (Garden City, N.Y.: Doubleday & Company, Inc., 1957), p. 3. 15. Ibid., p. 160. 16. Ibid., p. 194.

An Argument Against Bolshevist Ideals

M.D. Petre

Writing from France a few months after the publication of *Brave New World*, M.D. Petre found in it a perfect exposition of the ideals and philosophy of a young
Bolshevist of her acquaintance. The spiritual path of
Bolshevism, or Russian communism, she states, is incompatible with Christianity. The decision to choose
which spiritual path to follow cannot be made by argument, she points out, and she finds in the novel a
warning about the consequences of choosing the Bolshevist path. Petre wrote essays on the philosophy of
religion.

Controversy is not, I take it, very much of the spirit of our
age. Controversy, of course, there is, and controversy most
probably there will always be, but I think we all realise, better than we did, that it is by choice, and not by argument,
that the great questions of life are decided; and that choice is
even, in its way, a more powerful apology than the closest
chain of reasoning can offer.

Very particularly does this seem to me the case in regard
to one of the greatest political and spiritual struggles which
the world has ever known, that between the customs, the
ideals, the systems and the faith of the world as we have
known it until now, and those of a new society which is in
process of self-creation.

Most eyes are foolishly turned to the political character of
the contest between our old Western civilisation and Bolshevism. But at long last it is the spiritual conflict which will
most vitally affect the destiny of mankind. And controversy
is here more or less useless, it is a choice that mankind has
to make. Absolute truth is neither on one side nor on the
other; every human system and every Church is a means

Excerpted from M.D. Petre, "Bolshevist Ideals and the 'Brave New World,'" *The Hibbert
Journal*, October 1932.

and not an end. But a means to what? And here comes the great distinction. What is the end proposed by either system? In other words, what is the purpose of human life?

So that every social and religious system has to be estimated, first, according to its conception of the main purpose of life; secondly, according to its aptitude for the attainment of that purpose. We may have religions and systems that agree as to the meaning and end of life but differ as to the means of fulfilment; and we can have religions and systems that differ on the first question, that oppose each other on the fundamental question of the whole meaning and purpose of life. And this is the basic opposition of which we are now the witnesses; the opposition between the new political and social system of Bolshevist Russia, and the political and social system of all our old civilisations. But far, far deeper, far more uncompromising, far fiercer is the religious and spiritual opposition between the two systems and conceptions of life than any mere social difference. . . .

A War to the Death Between Rival Religions

A religion it very truly is, but of a character so definite and distinct, and of dogmas so strange to the mentality of most of us, that it is not surprising if the majority of us fail to perceive that it is a religion at all. And yet, right back through the history of mankind, with its rival sects and warfares, there has, perhaps, never been a religious struggle more terrific than that which is now to be waged. For Christianity and Paganism, Christianity and Mahometanism [Islam], Catholicism and Protestantism, have always had deep-lying common principles beneath all their vital differences; they were all turned, even Paganism, to the Beyond; they all upheld personal values and personal relationships, and some doctrine of personal salvation. Here we have a religion with no Beyond—a religion that ignores the question of personal salvation. It is also a religion without a God, but not the first comer in that respect. Buddhism is a religion without a God, and so was Comtism, and yet can we deny the appellation of religion to either of them? Some, I know, would exclaim that there was no religion without a God. We may agree that there is no true one without a God—but we cannot go further than this. The etymology of the word, to which appeal is so often made, indicates the contrary. Where there is worship, sacrifice and service there is religion, and all three find their place in the creed of Bolshevism. These religious acts do indeed differ by reason of the difference of their object, but their character remains. And once we accept the fact that Bolshevism is in very fact a religion we shall, on the one hand, better explain, even in some sense excuse, its violence, and, on the other hand, we shall probably become more ardent in our spiritual opposition to this living and not merely negative enemy of our own religion. We shall understand it better, we shall perhaps dislike it more. For, at long last, many religions have learned to live together, side by side, but it would be impossible for Bolshevism and Christianity thus to co-exist; it must, so far as one can see, be a war to the death between them.

I could, perhaps, never have written these pages had I not chanced to come, for a passing period, into contact with a genuine living product of Bolshevist philosophy; a young mind that had been early soaked in its principles, till they had become as natural and, apparently, inevitable as the main truths of Christianity to a born and convinced Christian. I quickly found in our discussions that I was continually taking for granted exactly those things which he definitely excluded from his philosophy of life, so that our differences were so profound that we were both of us sometimes unconscious of them, and were arguing merely on surface questions. We differed in our sense of duty, we differed in our respective forms of self-love; we differed as to our origin, we differed still more as to our end; we professed submission to totally different masters, though we were both equally firm in our allegiance.

I found in this young Bolshevist such a renunciation of individual claims as could only be equalled by the highest types of sanctity amongst Christians, and yet that self-renunciation is, in the two cases, of a totally different character. The renunciation of the Christian consists in wilful self-sacrifice; he gives himself to God, he gives himself to his fellow-men, and puts himself and all that he has at their service. The renunciation of the perfect Bolshevist, or Communist, could not properly be termed self-sacrifice; he does not give himself, but he is taken; he allows himself to be taken, and his sacrifice is completed by his whole-hearted acceptance of his fate. If one were to employ theological terms to describe the subject, one would say that it would be a form of blasphemy, according to the Bolshevist creed, to speak of his renunciation as self-sacrifice; he is too wholly a part of the living mechanism, for and by which he exists, to be capable of wilful self-sacrifice. His subjugation to that which, for him, takes the place of God is complete. The immediate recipient of his self-renunciation is the State of which he is politically a member; but the ultimate recipient, the real substitute for the Christian God, is collective humanity. There is an absoluteness, an inevitableness in this relationship of the individual to society which there cannot be where the notion of personal relationships prevails. There can be here no difference of merit and degree; the claim is total on the one side, the submission must be total on the other. . . .

NO IMPERFECTION ALLOWED

Bolshevism allows of no imperfection in its system, and since it is wholly of this earth it can not only demand, but can also ensure obedience. Its rule is absolute and uncompromising, and it is not hampered in its action, like the Christian Church, by the doctrine of conscience. There is no Christian Church but will admit that the conscience of each man is the final tribunal to which his belief and conduct must be referred. But for Bolshevism the conscience is collective and no one has a right to prefer his own standard of conduct. I think it is difficult for us, who are saturated with the notion of spiritual and personal liberty, to realise how overwhelming may be the domination of a contrary conception, and how absolutely it might subjugate the minds of those educated under that system. Perhaps the modern mind of the Western Christian does not fully understand how much the doctrine of personal liberty in thought and action depends on the belief in a spiritual Beyond and on the faith in God, whatever our idea of Him may be. The setting of time in eternity lifts the things of time to a higher responsibility and the sense of a higher tribunal to which recourse can be had softens—even weakens—the otherwise ruthless character of human justice. It feels that its rights are circumscribed.

Bolshevism has no sense of any limiting or transcending power above itself; it claims to be the ruler, the Providence, the life and the end of all its members. Liberty may be exercised within its bounds but not outside them. It ensures to its people probably less suffering than Christianity, but also less joy, for joy, like suffering, has a personal character. It eliminates tragedy, which implies the play of great passions, and the clash of great wills, and in place of it inculcates unbounded endurance. The members of the Bolshevist religion will seldom complain, but neither will they rejoice. They will adore, for worship is one of the main acts of religion; but their adoration will be that of subjects and not of children. It will not be so much the adoration offered by inferiors, as that of mere elements of a whole to that whole itself. They will not so much sacrifice as be sacrificed; they will be rather as Isaac than as Christ. And they will serve with body and soul, because for that alone they exist. It is as a whole that Bolshevism will claim to be estimated; its religion is one of collectivism, and personal criticisms are vain.

THE BOLSHEVIST PHILOSOPHY IN *BRAVE NEW WORLD*

With what wonder and admiration, some time after forming and writing these impressions, I took up Mr Aldous Huxley's amazing story of a world wherein the ideals of Bolshevist philosophy should be fantastically and impossibly fulfilled. Not often has anyone achieved the difficult task of presenting in imaginative form the social results of any philosophy, with such fine point and marvellous realism as we find in *Brave New World.* The author is, I trust, amused and not exasperated by the utter misunderstanding on the part of many; such misunderstanding is as inevitable as the common misunderstanding of Bolshevism itself.

The first characteristic of the *Brave New World* is its universal contentment and happiness.

"Is not that enough?" a good many will exclaim. Well, perhaps for some it will appear enough, but let each one think well and take his choice. All classes of the Brave New World, into which a strict system of Caste has been introduced, are happy because they have been shaped, pre-natally and post-natally, to be entirely satisfied with their allotted part in life, and to consider themselves entirely happy.

As to this Caste system which Mr Huxley has introduced into his scheme, he is probably severely criticised by Bolshevist philosophers for supposing it to be an element of their system. But he has divined, and with some likelihood of being right, that something of the kind would be almost essential to a complete fulfilment of the social ideals of Bolshevism.

We have, therefore, a world divided into a certain number of classes, in each of which the individuals have been so "conditioned" that they can only be happy in the state to which society has destined them. Physically and mentally they are formed for their particular lot in life.

> "I'm glad I'm not an Epsilon," said Lenina with conviction.
>
> "And if you were an Epsilon," said Henry, "your conditioning would have made you no less thankful that you weren't a Beta or an Alpha.". . .
>
> "And that," put in the Director sententiously, "that is the secret of happiness and virtue—liking what you've *got* to do. All conditioning aims at that: making people like their unescapable social destiny."

The hair-raising description of how babies are taught not to love flowers shows us one of the "conditioning" processes. . . .

DOING AWAY WITH "USELESS" KNOWLEDGE

Certain departments of knowledge are to be deemed useless or pernicious even to the higher classes of the community. Above all *history*—and if any of my readers have chanced to peruse some of the latest pamphlets on Bolshevist education they will have been impressed by the small part that history occupies. . . . For Bolshevists are as severe in their censorship as was ever a Spanish Inquisitor. If we want to form a totally new world we must cut away the roots of the past; we must be as though we were freshly made and owed nothing to what has gone before.

> "History is bunk," said the Director. He waved his hand; and it was as though, with an invisible feather whisk, he had brushed away a little dust, and the dust was Harappa, was Ur of the Chaldees; some spider-webs, and they were Thebes and Babylon and Cnossus and Mycenae. Whisk, whisk and where was Odysseus, where was Job, where were Jupiter and Gotama and Jesus? Whisk—and those spectres of antique dust called Athens and Rome, Jerusalem and the Middle Kingdom. Whisk—the place where Italy had been was empty. Whisk, the cathedrals; whisk, whisk, King Lear and the Thoughts of Pascal. Whisk Passion; whisk Requiem; whisk Symphony; whisk . . .

But it is not only history that must be dropped out of the educational curriculum. What about Art, what about Science, if they should be allowed to get their heads? And, above all, love? Of what system-wrecking follies is it not capable? Parental and filial love have been eliminated by the elimination of parents and children; the love of lovers is eliminated by making of it a pastime, a sport, an enthralling game, but not an attachment or a passion. . . .

And as to science, she too must be harnessed and controlled.

"It isn't only art that's incompatible with happiness," says Mustapha Mond, one of the world controllers. (He himself is something in the nature of an unbelieving Pope; he sees beyond his own system but cynically and sceptically adheres to it). "It's also science. Science is dangerous. . . . I was a pretty good physicist in my time. . . . Too good . . ."

But finally, he says: "I preferred this . . . I was given the choice: to be sent to an island, where I could have got on with my pure science or to be taken on to the Controllers' Council, with the prospect of succeeding in due course to an actual Controllership. I chose this and let the science go."

Of course science is a danger, in a lesser degree than God, but still in its own degree. For there is the science which ministers to the needs of man, and this is not only harmless, but even beneficial. But there is also the science that spreads its wings for the beyond, and that may, perchance, return to the Ark with a sprig of hope in its mouth, with a message from the Beyond, a sign from God to man.

Stability and happiness; these are the two ruling aims of the State; nothing must disturb the general equilibrium, nor ruffle the general contentment.

Very cleverly has Mr Huxley introduced into his scheme the two malcontents. Bernard Marx, a poor creature, not at all better than those around him, but restless because he is a misfit. Helmholz, ill at ease in the system because he feels that there is something lacking, and that which is lacking is, of course, his own soul and his own individuality.

> "Did you ever feel," he asked, "as though you had something inside you that was only waiting for you to give it a chance to come out? Some sort of extra power that you aren't using. You know, like all the water that goes down the falls instead of through the turbines."

And into the midst of it all walks the *Savage*, ignorant of everything but the poetry of Shakespeare; crude, uneducated, foolish and violent. He is helpless and yet invincible; helpless in a system to which he has not been conditioned; invincible by reason of that individuality which he alone, amongst them all, possesses.

The late Russian historian Pokrovsky denied the influence of personalities, "instruments which in time to come may be artificially made as to-day we make electric accumulators."[1]

Mr Huxley has given us an imaginative fulfilment of this prediction; and the Savage has the weakness and the strength of a personality not "artificially made." He wants to love, but to love for ever. He wants to work, but to work with effort and in the sweat of his brow. He wants to live, but to live dangerously. He wants to rejoice, but he wants also to suffer. He wants life with its fulness, but he wants also death with its tragedy. All the wonders of material civilisation leave him cold. . . .

A Call to Choice

And so he passes through the *Brave New World* and passes out, unaffected by it and unaffecting; as tragically unhappy as the rest of them are mechanically happy; as useless to them as they are useless to him. It is a wonderful story, and, as I said at the beginning of this article, it is a call not to argument and controversy but to choice.

> Call it the fault of civilisation. God isn't compatible with machinery and scientific medicine and universal happiness. You must make your choice. Our civilisation has chosen machinery and medicine and happiness. That's why I have to keep these books locked up in the safe.

Of course God Himself may eventually have something to say to it, but Mr Aldous Huxley's picture is of a world in which man has and pursues his own way. It is God who just makes all the difference, for without Him there is no personality, and without personality there is, for us, no God. We always knew that He is our Beginning and our End—from Bolshevism we have learned that He is above all, our Escape. For the soul that believes in God can escape through any human mesh; it cannot be contained in even the most rigorous and close-knit system. God is the Enemy of a Bolshevist theory of society, because God is an Escape.

And from Bolshevism we learn also that God is the one great principle of unity; that unity after which every living soul continually searches—whether in truth, or love, or goodness. The denizens of the Brave New World form a collectivity, but not an unity. They have no link with past or

1. From obituary notice in *The (London) Times.*

future; no sorrow for the dead, no love for the coming generations—they live together in perfect agreement, because where there is no principle of unity neither is there any principle of division.

> The world's stable now. People are happy; they get what they want, and they never want what they can't get. They're well off; they're safe; they're never ill; they're not afraid of death; they're blissfully ignorant of passion and old age; they're plagued with no fathers or mothers; they've got no wives, or children, or lovers to feel strongly about; they're so conditioned that they practically can't help behaving as they ought to behave.

And as to God: "He manifests Himself as an absence, as though He weren't there at all."

So that we cannot help hoping that the last word, after all, will rest with Him.

It is a very remarkable book, and I leave it with the wish that its meaning may not be lessened by further treatment in theatre or cinema.

And as to Bolshevism, with regard to which there is so much more to be said. Will it achieve success even according to its own aims? Will the suppression of individual values, the limitation of human aims to this earth and all that this earth can give us, contribute, at last, to fuller prosperity even in this world?

Bolshevism is not an irreligion, but a religion, and the war in front of us is a mighty one, and one to the death.

The Author's Second Thoughts

Aldous Huxley

In 1946, fourteen years after the publication of *Brave New World*, Huxley was invited to write a new foreword to the novel. The world had just emerged from World War II; although this does not provoke a hopeful response in the author, he does explain why *Brave New World* made no mention of atomic energy—the explosive force whose power was demonstrated in Hiroshima in the final days of the war. Huxley finds that the world he predicted is approaching much faster than he had originally imagined it might; in fact, much of the basis necessary to make people love their servitude is already in place. Taking note of increased divorce rates, especially in America, Huxley suggests that sexual freedom, "in conjunction with the freedom to daydream under the influence of dope and movies and the radio, . . . will help to reconcile [a dictator's] subjects to the servitude which is their fate." The world he describes in *Brave New World*, he says, might be only three or four generations away.

Chronic remorse, as all the moralists are agreed, is a most undesirable sentiment. If you have behaved badly, repent, make what amends you can and address yourself to the task of behaving better next time. On no account brood over your wrongdoing. Rolling in the muck is not the best way of getting clean.

Art also has its morality, and many of the rules of this morality are the same as, or at least analogous to, the rules of ordinary ethics. Remorse, for example, is as undesirable in relation to our bad art as it is in relation to our bad behaviour. The badness should be hunted out, acknowledged and, if possible, avoided in the future. To pore over the liter-

Reprinted from the Foreword to *Brave New World*, by Aldous Huxley. Copyright 1932, 1960 by Aldous Huxley. Reprinted by permission of HarperCollins Publishers, Chatto & Windus Ltd., and Mrs. Laura Huxley.

ary shortcomings of twenty years ago, to attempt to patch a faulty work into the perfection it missed at its first execution, to spend one's middle age in trying to mend the artistic sins committed and bequeathed by the different person who was oneself in youth—all this is surely vain and futile. And that is why this new *Brave New World* is the same as the old one. Its defects as a work of art are considerable; but in order to correct them I should have to rewrite the book—and in the process of rewriting, as an older, other person, I should probably get rid not only of some of the faults of the story, but also of such merits as it originally possessed. And so, resisting the temptation to wallow in artistic remorse, I prefer to leave both well and ill alone and to think about something else.

In the meantime, however, it seems worthwhile at least to mention the most serious defect in the story, which is this. The Savage is offered only two alternatives, an insane life in Utopia, or the life of a primitive in an Indian village, a life more human in some respects, but in others hardly less queer and abnormal. At the time the book was written this idea, that human beings are given free will in order to choose between insanity on the one hand and lunacy on the other, was one that I found amusing and regarded as quite possibly true. For the sake, however, of dramatic effect, the Savage is often permitted to speak more rationally than his upbringing among the practitioners of a religion that is half fertility cult and half *Penitente* ferocity would actually warrant. Even his acquaintance with Shakespeare would not in reality justify such utterances. And at the close, of course, he is made to retreat from sanity; his native *Penitente*-ism reasserts its authority and he ends in maniacal self-torture and despairing suicide. "And so they died miserably ever after"— much to the reassurance of the amused, Pyrrhonic aesthete who was the author of the fable.

Today I feel no wish to demonstrate that sanity is impossible. On the contrary, though I remain no less sadly certain than in the past that sanity is a rather rare phenomenon, I am convinced that it can be achieved and would like to see more of it. For having said so in several recent books and, above all, for having compiled an anthology of what the sane have said about sanity and the means whereby it can be achieved, I have been told by an eminent academic critic that I am a sad symptom of the failure of an intellectual class in time of crisis. The

implication being, I suppose, that the professor and his col-
leagues are hilarious symptoms of success. The benefactors of
humanity deserve due honour and commemoration. Let us
build a Pantheon for professors. It should be located among
the ruins of one of the gutted cities of Europe or Japan, and
over the entrance to the ossuary I would inscribe, in letters six
or seven feet high, the simple words: SACRED TO THE MEMORY OF
THE WORLD'S EDUCATORS. SI MOMUMENTUM REQUIRIS
CIRCUMSPICE.

But to return to the future . . . If I were now to rewrite the
book, I would offer the Savage a third alternative. Between
the utopian and the primitive horns of his dilemma would
lie the possibility of sanity—a possibility already actualized, to
some extent, in a community of exiles and refugees from the
Brave New World, living within the borders of the Reservation.
In this community economics would be decentralist and
Henry-Georgian, politics Kropotkinesque co-operative. Science
and technology would be used as though, like the Sabbath, they
had been made for man, not (as at the present and still more so
in the Brave New World) as though man were to be adapted
and enslaved to them. Religion would be the conscious and intelligent pursuit of man's Final End, the unitive knowledge of
the immanent Tao or Logos, the transcendent Godhead or
Brahman. And the prevailing philosophy of life would be a kind
of Higher Utilitarianism, in which the Greatest Happiness principle would be secondary to the Final End principle—the first
question to be asked and answered in every contingency of life
being: "How will this thought or action contribute to, or interfere with, the achievement, by me and the greatest possible
number of other individuals, of man's Final End?"

Brought up among the primitives, the Savage (in this hypothetical new version of the book) would not be transported to
Utopia until he had had an opportunity of learning something
at first hand about the nature of a society composed of freely
co-operating individuals devoted to the pursuit of sanity. Thus
altered, *Brave New World* would possess artistic and (if it is
permissible to use so large a word in connection with a work
of fiction) a philosophical completeness, which in its present
form it evidently lacks.

But *Brave New World* is a book about the future and, whatever its artistic or philosophical qualities, a book about the future can interest us only if its prophecies look as though they
might conceivably come true. From our present vantage point,

fifteen years further down the inclined plane of modern history, how plausible do its prognostications seem? What has happened in the painful interval to confirm or invalidate the forecasts of 1931?

One vast and obvious failure of foresight is immediately apparent. *Brave New World* contains no reference to nuclear fission. That it does not is actually rather odd, for the possibilities of atomic energy had been a popular topic of conversation for years before the book was written. My old friend, Robert Nichols, had even written a successful play about the subject, and I recall that I myself had casually mentioned it in a novel published in the late twenties. So it seems, as I say, very odd that the rockets and helicopters of the seventh century of Our Ford should not have been powered by disintegrating nuclei. The oversight may not be excusable; but at least it can be easily explained. The theme of *Brave New World* is not the advancement of science as such; it is the advancement of science as it affects human individuals. The triumphs of physics, chemistry and engineering are tacitly taken for granted. The only scientific advances to be specifically described are those involving the application to human beings of the results of future research in biology, physiology and psychology. It is only by means of the sciences of life that the quality of life can be radically changed. The sciences of matter can be applied in such a way that they will destroy life or make the living of it impossibly complex and uncomfortable; but, unless used as instruments by the biologists and psychologists, they can do nothing to modify the natural forms and expressions of life itself. The release of atomic energy marks a great revolution in human history, but not (unless we blow ourselves to bits and so put an end to history) the final and most searching revolution.

This really revolutionary revolution is to be achieved, not in the external world, but in the souls and flesh of human beings. Living as he did in a revolutionary period, the Marquis de Sade very naturally made use of this theory of revolutions in order to rationalize his peculiar brand of insanity. Robespierre had achieved the most superficial kind of revolution, the political. Going a little deeper, Babeuf had attempted the economic revolution. Sade regarded himself as the apostle of the truly revolutionary revolution, beyond mere politics and economics— the revolution in individual men, women and children, whose bodies were henceforward to become the common sexual property of all and whose minds were to be purged of all the natural decencies, all the laboriously acquired inhibitions of traditional civilization. Between sadism and the really revolutionary revolution there is, of course, no necessary or inevitable connection. Sade was a lunatic and the more or less conscious goal of his revolution was universal chaos and destruction. The people who govern the Brave New World may not be sane (in what may be called the absolute sense of the word); but they are not madmen, and their aim is not anarchy but social stability. It is in order to achieve stability that they carry out, by scientific means, the ultimate, personal, really revolutionary revolution.

But meanwhile we are in the first phase of what is perhaps the penultimate revolution. Its next phase may be atomic warfare, in which case we do not have to bother with prophecies about the future. But it is conceivable that we may have enough sense, if not to stop fighting altogether, at least to behave as rationally as did our eighteenth-century ancestors. The unimaginable horrors of the Thirty Years War actually taught men a lesson, and for more than a hundred years the politicians and generals of Europe consciously resisted the temptation to use their military resources to the limits of destructiveness or (in the majority of conflicts) to go on fighting until the enemy was totally annihilated. They were aggressors, of course, greedy for profit and glory; but they were also conservatives, determined at all costs to keep their world intact, as a going concern. For the last thirty years there have been no conservatives; there have been only nationalistic radicals of the right and nationalistic radicals of the left. The last conservative statesman was the fifth Marquess of Lansdowne; and when he wrote a letter to the *Times*, suggesting that the First World War should be concluded with a compromise, as most of the wars of the eighteenth century had been, the editor of that once conservative journal refused to print it. The nationalistic radicals had their way, with the consequences that we all know—Bolshevism, Fascism, inflation, depression, Hitler, the Second World War, the ruin of Europe and all but universal famine.

Assuming, then, that we are capable of learning as much from Hiroshima as our forefathers learned from Magdeburg, we may look forward to a period, not indeed of peace, but of limited and only partially ruinous warfare. During that period it may be assumed that nuclear energy will be harnessed to industrial uses. The result, pretty obviously, will be a series of economic and social changes unprecedented in rapidity and completeness. All the existing patterns of human life will be disrupted and new patterns will have to be improvised to conform with the nonhuman fact of atomic power. Procrustes in modern dress, the nuclear scientist will prepare the bed on which mankind must lie; and if mankind doesn't fit—well, that will be just too bad for mankind. There will have to be some stretching and a bit of amputation—the same sort of stretching and amputations as have been going on ever since applied science really got into its stride, only this time they will be a good deal more drastic than in the past. These far from painless operations will be directed by highly centralized totalitarian governments. Inevitably so; for the immediate future is likely to resemble the immediate past, and in the immediate past rapid technological changes, taking place in a mass-producing economy and among a population predominantly propertyless, have always tended to produce economic and social confusion. To deal with confusion, power has been centralized and government control increased. It is probable that all the world's governments will be more or less completely totalitarian even before the harnessing of atomic energy; that they will be totalitarian during and after the harnessing seems almost certain. Only a large-scale popular movement toward decentralization and self-help can arrest the present tendency toward statism. At present there is no sign that such a movement will take place.

There is, of course, no reason why the new totalitarianisms should resemble the old. Government by clubs and firing squads, by artificial famine, mass imprisonment and mass deportation, is not merely inhumane (nobody cares much about that nowadays), it is demonstrably inefficient and in an age of advanced technology, inefficiency is the sin against the Holy Ghost. A really efficient totalitarian state would be one in which the all-powerful executive of political bosses and their army of managers control a population of slaves who do not have to be coerced, because they love their servitude. To make them love it is the task assigned, in present-day totalitarian states, to ministries of propaganda, newspaper editors and schoolteachers. But their methods are still crude and unscientific. The old Jesuits' boast that, if they were given the schooling of the child, they could answer for the man's religious opinions, was a product of wishful thinking. And the modern pedagogue is probably rather less efficient at conditioning his pupils' reflexes than were the reverend fathers who educated Voltaire. The greatest triumphs of propaganda have been accomplished, not by doing something, but by refraining from doing. Great is truth, but still greater, from a practical point of view, is silence about truth. By simply not mentioning certain subjects, by lowering what Mr. Churchill calls an "iron curtain" between the masses and such facts or arguments as the local political bosses regard as undesirable, totalitarian propagandists have influenced opinion much more effectively than they could have done by the most eloquent denunciations, the most compelling of logical rebuttals. But silence is not enough. If persecution, liquidation and the other symptoms of social friction are to be avoided, the positive side of propaganda must be made as effective as the negative. The most important Manhattan Projects of the future will be vast government-sponsored enquiries into what the politicians and the participating scientists will call "the problem of happiness"—in other words, the problem of making people love their servitude. Without economic security, the love of servitude cannot possibly come into existence; for the sake of brevity, I assume that the all-powerful executive and its managers will succeed in solving the problem of permanent security. But security tends very quickly to be taken for granted. Its achievement is merely a superficial, external revolution. The love of servitude cannot be established except as the result of a deep, personal revolution in human minds and bodies. To bring about that revolution we require, among others, the following discoveries and inventions. First, a greatly improved technique of suggestion––through infant conditioning and, later, with the aid of drugs, such as scopolamine. Second, a fully developed science of human differences, enabling government managers to assign any given individual to his or her proper place in the social and economic hierarchy. (Round pegs in square holes tend to have dangerous thoughts about the social system and to infect others with their discontents.) Third (since reality, however utopian, is something from which people feel the need of taking pretty frequent holidays), a substitute for alcohol and the other narcotics, something at once less harmful and more pleasure-giving than gin or heroin. And fourth (but this would be a long-term project, which it would take generations of totalitarian control to bring to a successful conclusion) a foolproof system of eugenics, designed to standardize the human product and so to facilitate the task of the managers. In *Brave New World* this standardization of the human product has been pushed to fantastic, though not perhaps impossible, extremes. Technically and ideologically we are still a long way from bottled babies and Bokanovsky groups of semi-morons. But by A.F. 600, who knows what may not be happening? Meanwhile the other characteristic features of that happier and more stable world—the equivalents of soma and hypnopaedia and the scientific caste system—are probably not more than three or four generations away. Nor does the sexual promiscuity of *Brave New World* seem so very distant. There are already certain American cities in which the number of divorces is equal to the number of marriages. In a few years, no doubt, marriage licenses will be sold like dog licenses, good for a period of twelve months, with no law against changing dogs or keeping more than one animal at a time. As political and economic freedom diminishes, sexual freedom tends compensatingly to increase. And the dictator (unless he needs cannon fodder and families with which to colonize empty or conquered territories) will do well to encourage that freedom. In conjunction with the freedom to daydream under the influence of dope and movies and the radio, it will help to reconcile his subjects to the servitude which is their fate.

All things considered it looks as though Utopia were far closer to us than anyone, only fifteen years ago, could have imagined. Then, I projected it six hundred years into the future. Today it seems quite possible that the horror may be upon us within a single century. That is, if we refrain from blowing ourselves to smithereens in the interval. Indeed, unless we choose to decentralize and to use applied science, not as the end to which human beings are to be made the means, but as the means to producing a race of free individuals, we have only two alternatives to choose from: either a number of national, militarized totalitarianisms, having as their root the terror of the atomic bomb and as their consequence the destruction of civilization (or, if the warfare is limited, the perpetuation of militarism); or else one supra-national totalitarianism, called into existence by the social chaos resulting from rapid technological progress in general and the atomic revolution in particular, and developing, under the need for efficiency and stability, into the welfare-tyranny of Utopia. You pays your money and you takes your choice.

CHAPTER 2

Brave New World as Prophesy

READINGS ON
BRAVE NEW WORLD

Huxley's World Could Be Saved by Mutations

John Chamberlain

In this review of *Brave New World* from 1932, John Chamberlain finds Huxley's new novel an entertaining satire. Chamberlain faults Huxley on his understanding of biology, though, suggesting that even producing children in a laboratory is not foolproof. If a mutation affects just one child, it might produce a person who could destroy the static world the novelist portrays. Chamberlain, a career journalist, wrote books on capitalism and U.S. business history.

Dignity, beyond all else, has attended the creation of the classic Utopias, from that of Plato on down to Edward Bellamy's perfectly geared industrial machine. Conceived in kindliness of spirit, dedicated to the high future of the race and offered with becoming humility as contributions to the questionable science of human happiness, these classic Utopias have only too often seemed mere parodies of the Napoleonic State, the Taylor system of the laboratory where guinea pigs are bred to predestined fates. It has remained for Aldous Huxley to build the Utopia to end Utopias—or such Utopias as go to mechanics for their inspiration, at any rate. He has satirized the imminent spiritual trustification of mankind, and has made rowdy and impertinent sport of the World State whose motto shall be Community, Identity, Stability.

This slogan, Mr. Huxley seems to be saying under the noise made by his knockabout farce, is thoroughly unbiological. Mankind moves forward by stumbling—we almost said progressing—from one unstable equilibrium to another unstable equilibrium; and if the human animal ever ceases to do this he will go to the ant (the sluggard!) and become a hived creature. Mr. Huxley doesn't like the prospect. So here

51

we have him, as entertainingly atrabilious as ever he was in *Antic Hay* or *Point Counter Point*, mocking the Fords, the Hitlers, the Mussolinis, the Sir Alfred Monds, the Owen D. Youngs—all who would go back on laissez-faire and on toward the servile state. His Utopia has much in common with those of the nineteenth century—everything, in fact, but their informing and propulsive faith. It is as regimented as Etienne Cabet's Icaria, the communal Utopia seemingly made of breeding the bureaucracy of the first Napoleon with the ghostly positive of August Comte; and its ideas of dispensing *panem et circenses* [bread and circuses] to the populace are precisely those of Edward Bellamy's *Looking Backward*—only Mr. Huxley, who has had the opportunity to visit moving-picture emporium and radio studio, knows the difference between possibility and actuality in popular entertainment. With the Highland Park and River Rouge plants, the Foster and Catchings ideology of consumption, the Five-Year Plan, the synthetic creation of vitamins, the spectacle of a chicken heart that lives on without benefit of surrounding chicken, the flight of Post and Gatty and the control of diabetics all behind him in point of time, Mr. Huxley has had an easy task to turn the nineteenth century hope into a counsel of despair. And like an older utopian, Mr. Huxley finds no room for the poet in his Model T. world. His poets are all Emotional Engineers.

BRAVE NEW GADGETS

Behold, then, the gadget satirically enshrined. As Bellamy anticipated the radio in 1888, Mr. Huxley has foreseen the displacement of the talkie by the "feelie," a type of moving picture that will give tactile as well as visual and aural delight. Spearmint has given way to Sex Hormone gum—the favorite chew of one of Mr. Huxley's minor characters, Mr. Benito Hoover. Grammes of soma—a non-hangover-producing substitute for rum—are eaten daily by the populace; they drive away the blues. God had dissolved into Ford (sometimes called Freud), and the jingle goes "Ford's in his flivver, all's well with the world." Ford's book, *My Life and Work*, has become the new Bible. The Wurlitzer has been supplemented by the scent organ, which plays all the tunes from cinnamon to camphor, with occasional whiffs of kidney pudding for discord. Babies, of course, are born—or rather, decanted—in the laboratory; and by a process known

WHAT'S WRONG WITH UTOPIA?

In this 1932 review, Henry Hazlitt suggests that there is so much suffering and chaos in the world that the threat posed in Brave New World *is unlikely. In fact, he implies, the world would do well to aim toward the stability and comfort of Huxley's world, yet people must do so in the sad knowledge that their efforts will be futile.*

What is wrong with this Utopia? Mr. Huxley attempts to tell us by the device of introducing a "savage," brought up under other ideals on an Indian reservation, and having read that author unknown to the Model T Utopia, Shakespeare. In the admittedly violent and often irrational reactions of the "savage" we have the indictment of this civilization. Not only is there no place in it for love, for romance, for fidelity, for parental affection, there is no suffering in it, and hence absolutely no need of nobility and heroism. In such a society the tragedies of Shakespeare become not merely irrelevant, but literally meaningless. This Model T civilization is distinguished by supreme stability, comfort, and happiness, but these things can be purchased only at a price, and the price is a high one. Not merely art and religion are brought to a standstill, but science itself, lest it make discoveries that would be socially disturbing. Even one of the ten World Controllers is led to suspect the truth, though of course forbidding the publication, of a theory holding that the purpose of life is not the maintenance of well-being, but "some intensification and refining of consciousness, some enlargement of knowledge."

Brave New World is successful as a novel and as a satire; but one need not accept all its apparent implications. A little suffering, a little irrationality, a little division and chaos, are perhaps necessary ingredients of an ideal state, but there has probably never been a time when the world has not had an oversupply of them. Only when we have reduced them enormously will Mr. Huxley's central problem become a real problem. Meanwhile reformers can continue to strain every muscle in the quiet assurance of their own futility. They may, for example, form their Leagues of Nations, draw up their Kellogg Pacts and Nine-Power Treaties, and hold their disarmament conferences, in the calm confidence that a Japan will still brutally attack a China.

Henry Hazlitt, "What's Wrong with Utopia?," review of *Brave New World, The Nation,* February 17, 1932.

as the Bokanovsky one egg can be made to proliferate into ninety-six children, all of them identical in feature, form and brain power. The Bokanovsky groups are used to man the factories, work the mines, and so on; there can be no jealousy in a Bokanovsky group, for its ideal is like-mindedness. But if there is little jealousy in Mr. Huxley's world, there is still shame; a girl blushes to think of having children in the good old viviparous way. To obviate the possibility of childbirth, the girls—or such of them as are not born sterile Freemartins—are put through daily Malthusian Drill in their impressionable 'teens. Buttons have disappeared and children play games of "Hunt the Zipper."

We are introduced at the outset to the Director of Hatcheries and Conditioning for Central London, who takes us through his plant and explains the creation of the various castes: Alphas, Betas, Gammas, Deltas and Epsilons, each caste ranging from minus to plus. Before a child is turned over to his station in life, he is thoroughly conditioned, by injection of hypnopaedic wisdom during sleep, to like precisely what he has to like. But slips there are, even in the most mechanical of all possible worlds, and owing to some oversight—possibly the spilling of alcohol into the blood surrogate upon which he was fed in his prenatal days— Bernard Marx, Mr. Huxley's hero, is dissatisfied.

Bernard loves Lenina Crowne in a sort of old-fashioned romantic way. He longs for solitude a deux. So with her he takes the rocket for a vacation in the New Mexican savage reservation. By sheer coincidence, the Director of Hatcheries and Conditioning for Central London had spent a vacation once upon a time in this reservation; and had lost his girl, a Betaminus, in a sudden and confusing desert thunderstorm. Bernard, of course, runs upon the girl—now an old woman—and her son, John, the Savage, born viviparously. Quickly he gets into touch with Mustapha Mond, his Fordship, the Resident Controller for Western Europe. Shall be bring them back by rocket to London? His Fordship thinks furiously and decides in the positive; and for the sake of educating the populace, the Savage and his Mother are shot over to England.

ONE MUTATION COULD SHAKE THE WORLD'S FOUNDATIONS

It is Mr. Huxley's habit to be deadly in earnest. One feels that he is pointing a high moral lesson in satirizing Utopia. Yet it is a little difficult to take alarm, for, as the hell-diver sees not the mud, and the angle worm knows not the intricacies of the Einstein theory, so the inhabitants of Mr. Huxley's world could hardly be conscious of the satirical overtones of the Huxleyan prose. And the bogy of mass production seems a little overwrought, since the need for it as religion, in a world that could rigidly control its birth rate and in which no one could make any money out of advertising and selling, would be scarcely intelligible even to His Fordship. Finally, if Mr. Huxley is unduly bothered about the impending static world, let him go back to his biology and meditate on the possibility that even in laboratory-created children mutations might be inevitable. A highly mechanized world, yes; but it might breed one Rousseau to shake it to the foundations and send men back to the hills and the goatskins. Meanwhile, while we are waiting for *My Life and Work* to replace the Bible, *Brave New World* may divert us; it offers a stop-gap.

Huxley's Biology Is Perfectly Right

Joseph Needham

In May 1932 *Scrutiny*, a new quarterly review based in Cambridge, England, published its first issue. Its contents included a "Manifesto" in which the editors lamented the dissolution of standards for critical reviewers, and pledged to pay attention to both "the drift of civilization" and "the plight of the arts." The following essay met both criteria, as Joseph Needham, one of the leading biologists of his day, strongly proclaims that Huxley (who also came from a family of scientists) has gotten the science—biology and psychology as well as philosophy—exactly right. *Brave New World*, writes Needham, clearly shows what lies ahead, and it should be required reading especially for those who trust in science to save the world.

'Utopias' writes Prof. Berdiaev, in a passage which Mr. Huxley chooses for his motto 'appear to be much more realisable than we used to think. We are finding ourselves face to face with a far more awful question, how can we avoid their actualisation? For they can be made actual. Life is marching towards them. And perhaps a new period is beginning, a period when intelligent men will be wondering how they can avoid these utopias, and return to a society non-utopian, less perfect, but more free.' Mr. Huxley's book is indeed a brilliant commentary on this dismally true remark. It is as if a number of passages from Mr. Bertrand Russell's recent book *The Scientific Outlook* had burst into flower, and had rearranged themselves in patches of shining colour like maneating orchids in a tropical forest. Paul planted, Apollos watered, but who gave the increase in this case, we may well ask, for a more diabolical picture of society (as some would say) can never have been painted.

Reprinted from Joseph Needham, "Biology and Mr. Huxley," *Scrutiny*, May 1932, by permission of the Needham Research Institute, Cambridge, England.

A DUAL THEME

Mr. Huxley's theme, embellished though it is by every arti-
fice of that ingenuity of which he is master, is primarily
dual, one of its aspects being the power of autocratic dicta-
torship, and the other, the possibilities of this power when
given the resources of a really advanced biological engineering. The book opens with a long description of a human
embryo factory, where the eggs emitted by carefully tended
ovaries, are brought up in the way they should go by mass-
production methods on an endless conveyor belt moving
very slowly until at last the infants are 'decanted' one by one
into a highly civilised world. The methods of education by
continual suggestion and all the possibilities of conditional
reflexes are brilliantly described, and we are shown a world
where art and religion no longer exist, but in which an *absolutely* stable form of society has been achieved, firstly, by
sorting out the eggs into groups of known inherited characteristics and then setting each group, when adult, to do the
work for which it is fitted, and secondly by allowing 'unlimited copulation' (sterile, of course) and unlimited sexual
gratification of every kind. Here Mr. Huxley, whether consciously or not, has incorporated the views of many psychologists, e.g. Dr. Money Kyrle. In an extremely interesting
paper[1] Dr. Kyrle has suggested that social discontent, which
has always been the driving force in social change, is a
manifestation of the Oedipus complexes of the members of
society, and cannot be removed by economic means. With
decrease of sexual taboos, these psychologists suggest, there
would be a decrease of frustration and hence of that aggres-
sion which finds its outlet in religion, socialism, or more violent forms of demand for social change. This doctrine is indeed an extremely plausible one, and provides an answer to
the question of what the 'born' reformer is to do when the
ideal communist state, for instance, has been brought into
being. Supposing that we have what we regard as an ideal
state, how shall we ensure its continuance? Only, says Dr.
Kyrle, by removing the sexual taboos which make the 'born'
reformer. Accordingly, Mr. Huxley shows us the state of affairs when the attack on post- and pre-marital, and pre-
pubertal taboos has long succeeded. The erotic play of chil-

1. R.M. Kyrle *A Psychologist's Utopia* (Psyche, 1931. p. 48).

dren is encouraged, universal sexual relations are the rule, and indeed any sign of the beginning of a more deep and lasting affection is rebuked and stamped out, as being anti-social.

BIOLOGY AND LOVE WILL PREVENT THE BRAVE NEW WORLD HUXLEY PICTURED

While it suddenly seems the techniques needed to clone humans may be developed any day now, Lee M. Silver doubts that the ability will lead to the government control visualized in Brave New World. *Paul Raeburn, in his review of Silver's book* Remaking Eden, *suggests that love is a more powerful force than Huxley reckoned with.*

Lee M. Silver, the author of *Remaking Eden: Cloning and Beyond in a Brave New World* . . . argues that most ethical debates over genetic enhancement and reproduction will become moot, because parents will demand these new techniques and government will be powerless to intervene. According to Silver, that's where Aldous Huxley got it wrong. In *Brave New World*, Huxley describes state-run human hatcheries where embryos are produced according to government specifications. But that's not the way it will happen, Silver says. "What Huxley failed to understand, or refused to accept, was the driving force behind babymaking. It is individuals and couples who want to reproduce themselves in their own images."

Indeed, he continues, when the right of parents "to control every other aspect of their children's lives" is widely accepted, it is hard to argue against allowing them to shape their children's genetics. For example, it might, in fact, be unethical to deny parents the opportunity to eliminate disease genes in their children. In one of Silver's Princeton classes, 90 percent of the students said they were opposed to the use of genetic engineering on their children for any reason. When asked about a hypothetical gene enhancement that could prevent AIDS infection, half of them changed their minds. . . .

Silver offers one simple suggestion as a guideline for the use of these new technologies. There are "many paths that can be followed to reach the goal of having a child," he writes. And the validity of any of these paths should be judged "not by their intrinsic nature, but by the love that a parent gives to the child after she or he is born." Whether or not we can produce humans without heads, Silver seems to be saying, we ought be sure they have hearts.

Paul Raeburn, "The Copy Shop," *New York Times*, January 11, 1998.

But Mr. Huxley, of course, sees so clearly what the psychologists do not see, that such a world must give up not only war, but also spiritual conflicts of any kind, not only superstition, but also religion, not only literary criticism but also great creative art of whatever kind, not only economic chaos, but also all the beauty of the old traditional things, not only the hard and ugly parts of ethics, but the tender and beautiful parts too. And it may well be that only biologists and philosophers will really appreciate the full force of Mr. Huxley's remarkable book. For of course in the world at large, those persons, and there will be many, who do not approve of his 'utopia,' will say, we can't believe all this, the biology is all wrong, it couldn't happen. Unfortunately, what gives the biologist a sardonic smile as he reads it, is the fact that *the biology is perfectly right*, and Mr. Huxley has included nothing in his book but what might be regarded as legitimate extrapolations from knowledge and power that we already have. Successful experiments are even now being made in the cultivation of embryos of small mammals in vitro, and one of the most horrible of Mr. Huxley's predictions, the production of numerous low-grade workers of precisely identical genetic constitution from one egg, is perfectly possible. Armadillos, parasitic insects, and even sea-urchins, if treated in the right way, do it now, and it is only a matter of time before it will be done with mammalian eggs. Many of us admit that as we walk along the street we dislike nine faces out of ten, but suppose that one of the nine were repeated sixty times. Of course, the inhabitants of Mr. Huxley's utopia were used to it.

TENDENCIES LEADING TO THE BRAVE NEW WORLD

And it is just the same in the philosophical realm. We see already among us the tendencies which only require reasonable extrapolation to lead to Brave New World. Publicism, represented in its academic form by Mr. Wittgenstein and Prof. Schlick, and in its more popular form by Prof. Hogben and Mr. Sewell, urges that the concept of reality must be replaced by the concept of communicability. Now it is only in science that perfect communicability is attainable, and in other words, all that we can profitably say is, in the last resort, scientific propositions clarified by mathematical logic. To the realm of the Unspeakable, therefore, belong Ethics, Religion, Art, Artistic Criticism, and many other things. This point of view has a certain attraction and possesses, or can be made to possess, considerable plausibility, but in the end it has the effect of driving out Reason from the private incommunicable worlds of non-scientific experience. We are left with science as the only substratum for Reason, but what is worse, Philosophy or Metaphysics too is relegated to the realm of the Unspeakable, so that Science, which began as a special form of Philosophy, and which only retains its intellectually beneficial character if it retains its status as a special form of Philosophy, becomes nothing more nor less than the Mythology accompanying a Technique. And what will happen to the world in consequence is seen with perfect clearness both by Mr. Aldous Huxley and by Mr. Bertrand Russell. 'The scientific society in its pure form' says Mr. Russell 'is incompatible with the pursuit of truth, with love, with art, with spontaneous delight, with every ideal that men have hitherto cherished, save only possibly ascetic renunciation. It is not knowledge that is the source of these dangers. Knowledge is good and ignorance is evil; to this principle the lover of the world can admit no exception. Nor is it power in and for itself that is the source of danger. What is dangerous is power wielded for the sake of power, not power wielded for the sake of genuine good.'

Such considerations, of course, do not solve the problem, they only convince us that a problem exists. But Mr. Huxley's orchid-garden is itself an exemplification of the contention that knowledge is always good, for had it not been for his imaginative power, we should not have seen so clearly what lies at the far end of certain inviting paths. To his convincing searchlight, humanity (it is not too much to say) will always owe great debt, and it must be our part to get his book read by any of our friends who suppose that science alone can be the saviour of the world.

Utopia Isn't All It's Cracked Up to Be

William Matter

Huxley warns that the myth and the reality of utopias are very different, notes critic William Matter. While the goals of utopists—such as stability and happiness—seem laudable, when carried to their logical conclusions, they spell an end to freedom.

In an interview with a representative from the *Paris Review*, Aldous Huxley once commented that he began *Brave New World* as a parody of H.G. Wells's *Men Like Gods*.[1] But the novel thus initiated as a simple parody was altered and broadened by the creative process until, in 1932, Huxley published his masterpiece of dystopian fiction—an incisive, satiric attack upon twentieth-century man's sometimes ingenuous trust in progress through science and mechanization. *Brave New World* warns the reader that "perfection" of the state entails absolute social stability, and social stability entails the effacement of personal freedom. The pleasantries of Obstacle Golf, scent organs, sex-hormone chewing-gum, and other mindless diversions garishly mask the loss of the individual's right to feel.

The novel is set in the distant future, specifically 632 years After Ford. As the Huxleyan chronology indicates, conventional religious worship has been replaced by the celebration of Henry Ford, whose assembly lines greatly advanced progress through mechanization. Symbolically, the top portion of the cross has been removed to form the sign of the T— in honor of Ford's Model T. This change is indicative of the high esteem Huxley satirically accords to science and the machine in his society. The reader sees many such "improve-

1. *Writers at Work: The "Paris Review" Interviews*, intro. Van Wyck Books, 2d series (New York: Viking, 1963), p. 198.

Excerpted from William Matter, "On *Brave New World*," in *No Place Else: Explorations in Utopian and Dystopian Fiction*, edited by Eric S. Rabkin, Martin H. Greenberg, and Joseph D. Olander (Carbondale: Southern Illinois University Press, 1983). Copyright © 1983 by the Board of Trustees, Southern Illinois University. Reprinted by permission of the publisher. Quotations from *Brave New World* reprinted by permission of Laura Huxley, Chatto & Windus Ltd., and HarperCollins Publishers.

ments." For example, the story begins as the Director of Hatcheries and Conditioning escorts a group of students through the Central London Hatchery. The official explains the modern processes employed to produce children. Embryos, he tells the students, are created scientifically. Women who are not freemartins (sterile) donate ova to the state. The eggs are put in expertly prepared test tubes which provide an artificial environment better than mother herself. A withdrawal is made from the sperm bank, and life begins before the watchful eyes of the supervising workers. Children are not born in this new world; they are decanted. In fact, the word "mother," as a symbol of past decadent social structures, is considered to be horribly vulgar. The family unit in *Brave New World* has been dissolved because love, a dangerously powerful emotion, may threaten the security of the state. By establishing eugenic control and doing away with the family, Huxley adheres to a utopian tradition first espoused in Plato's *Republic* and followed by later utopian thinkers.

MASS-PRODUCED PEOPLE

And the family in Huxley's futuristic society is indeed defunct. Viviparity has been replaced by a procedure known as "Bokanovsky's Process": "One egg, one embryo, one adult—normality. But a bokanovskified egg will bud, will proliferate, will divide. From eight to ninety-six buds, and every bud will grow into a perfectly formed embryo, and every embryo into a full-sized adult. Making ninety-six human beings grow where only one grew before. Progress." Standardized humans are thereby produced in "uniform batches." Individuality must be repressed because it invites a malleable social structure. By providing identical physical attributes for as many as ninety-six different people, Bokanovsky's Process serves as an extremely important instrument of social stability. As in the *Republic*, which provided Huxley with a model of the authoritarian utopia, stability in A.F. 632 is frightfully important. The same techniques Ford used for the mass production of automobiles have finally been applied to people.

As soon as the developing embryo is taken from the test tube, it is subjected to a series of chemical treatments that govern its continued physical and mental development. If the product resulting from the union of science and nature is fortunate enough to be an "Alpha," his future is promising.

But even if his mental and physical structure is deliberately retarded so that he will have an intellect and a physique most suitable for repetitious, menial tasks, he feels no anger toward society. Each child is subjected to several years of psychological conditioning reminiscent of Plato's "necessary lies" and Pavlov's classical conditioning experiments with dogs. An object is presented to the child and paired with disturbing noises and electrical shock. Soon the infant learns to associate his fear of strident sounds and pain with the object: "Books and loud noises, flowers and electric shocks—already in the infant mind these couples were compromisingly linked; and after two hundred repetitions of the same or a similar lesson would be wedded indissolubly. What man has joined, nature is powerless to put asunder." Other training sessions are devoted to making the child happy with his social position; the secret of happiness and virtue, the reader learns, is "liking what you've *got* to do. All conditioning aims at that: making people like their unescapable social destiny." Plato also employs a less sophisticated kind of conditioning to reconcile people to their distinct social destinies.

In *Brave New World* the principle of hypnopaedia is used for this purpose. A sleeping child is exposed to hours of whispered messages which reinforce class distinctions: "Alpha children wear grey. They work much harder than we do, because they're so frightfully clever. I'm really awfully glad I'm a Beta, because I don't work so hard. And then we are much better than the Gammas and Deltas. Gammas are stupid. They all wear green, and Delta children wear khaki. Oh no, I *don't* want to play with Delta children." Thus infants are decanted, in Plato's terms, with constitutions of gold, silver, brass, or iron. Opportunity for the Alpha is golden, but for the dwarfed Gamma it is iron at best. Because of Bokanovsky's Process and hypnopaedia, the physical and psychological characteristics of lower-caste children are unvexed by individual differences. Like residents in many other utopias, they are clothed in identical uniforms. People are not only stable, they are products—like electric knives and vacuum cleaners.

PREVENTING EMOTION

After the Director explains the process of decanting and conditioning to the students, one of the ten World Controllers talks to them about a usually forbidden subject—history. Before Ford, he tells them, people believed in an omnipotent being known as "God." Then Ford, or Freud as he frequently preferred to be called, developed new theories of psychology, sexual behavior, and mechanization. As his ideas were gradually adopted, the antiquated concepts of motherhood, love, family living, and monogamy were abandoned. The thought of "Home Sweet Home," in fact, has become repugnant to Huxley's society. Speaking to the students, the Controller does his best to characterize that effete idea. "'Home, home—a few rooms, stiflingly over-inhabited by a man, by a periodically teeming woman, by a rabble of boys and girls of all ages. No air, no space; an understerilized prison; darkness, disease, and smells.'" In order that the students might fully grasp the agonizing implications of "home," the official continues his description: "'And home was as squalid psychically as physically. Physically, it was a rabbit hole, a midden, hot with the frictions of tightly packed life, reeking with emotion. What suffocating intimacies, what dangerous, insane, obscene relationships between the members of the family group!'" The Controller's powerful condemnation of the family unit and of emotion is strictly in the tradition of Plato, Lycurgus, Tommaso Campanella, and many other utopists. In A.F. 632, as in the upper class of the *Republic*, the social danger of unrequited love is avoided because "every one belongs to every one else." The family unit encourages ideas of "mine" and "not mine" and breeds strong emotions. Passions, in many utopian societies, are considered dangerous to stability and therefore antagonistic to the public good. The Controller stresses this idea to the students: "'No pains have been spared to make your lives emotionally easy—to preserve you, so far as that is possible, from having emotions at all.'"

In continuing the discussion of emotion and the family group, the Controller indicates that even before Ford there were a few exceptions to the generally odious home life. He mentions a much more pleasant scene that took place at one time among the "uncivilized" people of Samoa, on islands off the New Guinea coast: "'The tropical sunshine lay like warm honey on the naked bodies of children tumbling promiscuously among the hibiscus blossoms. Home was in any one of twenty palm-thatched houses.'" The idea of multi-homes— Mutual Adoption Clubs, Huxley later calls them—reappears in an expanded form in his utopian novel, *Island*.

FORFEITING CREATIVITY

Many thematic points found in *Brave New World* germinate in Huxley's philosophy and appear in a positive form in his *Island*. But *Brave New World* describes what Huxley fears may be man's future. He seeks to warn his readers that "utopia" must be avoided. For example, Huxley views the theory of planned obsolescence with profound displeasure; but both children and adults in A.F. 632 are conditioned to believe that "ending is better than mending." The Controller does not approve any toy for distribution to the public unless it contains at least as many moving parts as the most complicated toys on the market. In that way, toys become obsolete very rapidly, and the demand for new and more complex forms of entertainment is always high. Here Huxley satirizes late nineteenth-century utopists like Edward Bellamy and Wells rather than the classical utopist who wishes to avoid luxury and material possessions. Thus it is apparent, even early in the novel, that the repetition of trite phrases from conditioning exercises, the inescapable togetherness, and the scientific "advances" are not intended by the author as goals toward which society should strive. By propounding a philosophy abhorrent to free men, Huxley shows his readers that the creative spirit—the right to think and act as individuals—must be forfeited if mankind follows his machines into utopia.

Huxley's beliefs subtend his brave new society, but he allows a few characters to experience moments of sanity even in A.F. 632. Some isolated individuals do not agree that as long as Ford is in his flivver all is well with the world. Bernard, an unusually small Alpha-Plus with eccentric habits, does not deem credible the assertion that "when the individual feels, the community reels." His highly typical and very "pneumatic" companion, Lenina, regards his rather unorthodox ideas as curious in the extreme. Talking about contemplating the sea alone, without the distraction of other people, Bernard confides: "'It makes me feel as though . . . I were more *me*, if you see what I mean. More on my own, not so completely a part of something else. Not just a cell in the social body. Doesn't it make you feel that, Lenina?'" But Bernard's blasphemies succeed only in making Lenina cry: "'It's horrible, it's horrible . . . and how can you talk like that about not wanting to be a part of the social body? After all, every one works for every one else.'" The same spirit of working for the state while ignoring one's individuality—a spirit that pervades the atmosphere of utopias by Plato, More, Campanella, Cabet, Bellamy, Howells, Wells, and others—is patently manifest in *Brave New World*. The "normal" member of society can neither accept nor understand Bernard's desire to be more than a single cell in a large social body.

DEATH HAS LITTLE MEANING

It is one thing to actively seek isolation as Bernard sometimes does, but it is quite another thing to find that a sense of alienation constantly and involuntarily invades one's happy moments. When Bernard and Lenina travel to the "Savage Reservation" in America, they encounter a peculiar young man named John who is atypical of reservation inhabitants. The Indians on the reservation are dark-skinned; but John . . . is fair-skinned and blond. He is different from the Indians in another respect, too. He is the son of a Beta-Minus from the outside world. His mother somehow forgot her contraceptives and exercises and became pregnant. She was stranded on the reservation and thus forced into viviparity. John, whom the civilized world outside the reservation calls the "Savage," does not fit within the society of the reservation. He is what Colin Wilson calls an "outsider."[2] The question of death bothers John. Like the existentialist, he sees that there is only one short step between the frightening, incomprehensible life of an outsider and the eternal quiet of nonexistence.

His hopes for happiness increase, however, when Bernard promises to take him from the reservation out into the brave new world. Through his mother's glowing accounts of life in civilized society, the Savage has learned about a euphoric drug called *soma*, throw-away clothes, music from synthetic plants, decanting, and many other modern advances in technology and social theory. He has also learned about life from a volume of Shakespeare's works, and he is anxious to escape the reservation to discover how accurately Shakespeare describes the human character. But when John actually gains entry into "civilized" society, he is surprised and distressed by what he finds. There is no love

2. For a detailed description of the plight of the isolated man, see Colin Wilson's *The Outsider* (New York: Delta, 1967).

as there is in Shakespeare; no one is allowed to be an individual. After seeing a large group of ugly, terrifying, identically dwarfed factory workers, John repeats Miranda's words with a very Huxleyan note of satire: "'O brave new world that has such people in it.'" He cannot understand a society which prefers Obstacle Golf to the dignity of man.

The people of England find John intensely interesting but equally confusing and frequently laughable. Bernard, whose social status has dramatically increased due to his association with John, parades him from one party to another until isolation seems a desirable goal. The question of death again becomes important to the Savage when he learns that his mother is dying. He is troubled because death means very little in A.F. 632. Children are conditioned to it: "Every tot spends two mornings a week in a Hospital for the Dying. All the best toys are kept there, and they get chocolate cream on death days. They learn to take dying as a matter of course." Individuals are considered useful to the state even after death, since phosphorus recovered in the process of cremation helps plants grow. The Savage, though, reacts quite differently to the idea of death. When his mother expires in a *soma* stupor, John rebels against the new world: "He woke once more to external reality, looked round him, knew what he saw—knew it, with a sinking sense of horror and disgust, for the recurrent delirium of his days and nights, the nightmare of swarming indistinguishable sameness." He preaches against the evils of *soma* to a group of Deltas about to get their weekly supply: "'Don't you want to be free and men? Don't you even understand what manhood and freedom are?'" The Savage's battle against *soma* and society is, of course, hopeless. The Deltas have been conditioned not to know what real freedom is. Reacting to this wild stranger, the befuddled men in khaki riot, and John is arrested. He is taken to the leader of the society, Mustapha Mond, who is one of the ten World Controllers. The philosophical debate between the Savage and Mond which ensues is, perhaps, the most important thematic point in *Brave New World*.

GOD, KNOWLEDGE, TRUTH, AND SCIENTIFIC PROGRESS ARE INCOMPATIBLE WITH UTOPIA

John is distressed because there is no concept of God in the new world. Mustapha Mond answers that "'God isn't compatible with machinery and scientific medicine and universal happiness. You must make your choice. Our civilization has chosen machinery and medicine and happiness.'" Science has, in fact, taken Huxley's civilization to the extreme position of making unhappiness a crime against the social body. Even scientists have been forced to make concessions for the sake of stability. Referring to a contemporary attitude Huxley regards as foolish, Mond states: "'It's curious . . . to read what people in the time of Our Ford used to write about scientific progress. They seemed to have imagined that it could be allowed to go on indefinitely, regardless of everything else. Knowledge was the highest good, truth the supreme value; all the rest was secondary and subordinate.'" Mond points out that science's good work must not be undone by unlimited research. An uncompromising devotion to knowledge and truth is harmful to stability. In this conversation between Mond and the Savage, Huxley condemns uncontrolled mechanization as dangerous even to the generally detestable society of *Brave New World*; he underlines the naiveté of writers who believe that science in utopia can go unchecked. Practical, controlled mechanization is the god of Huxley's perverse society, with Ford as the reigning deity.

The Savage does not care for talk of science and predestined happiness. He prefers the nobility and sacrifice of Shakespeare's world. He cannot accept any philosophy based upon hedonism and the social good. Life in this new world, he feels, is meaningless; there is nothing "brave" about it. To the Savage, the civilized infantility is "not expensive enough." John wants to feel intensely, to test the boundaries of his emotional faculties, and to live life fully. He seeks experiences involving pain and danger. The criticism of utopia which Huxley voices here is plain. The utopist generally makes every provision to be certain the inhabitants of his perfect world do not undergo disturbing emotions. Utopian writers like Plato and Campanella attempt to banish emotion altogether. The Savage, however, regards the experience of pain and sorrow as a valuable counterpoint to happiness. Such experiences are not possible in Mustapha Mond's world. The Controller makes this point very clear:

"And if ever, by some unlucky chance, anything unpleasant should somehow happen, why there's always *soma* to give you a holiday from the facts. And there's always *soma* to calm your anger, to reconcile you to your enemies, to make you patient and long-suffering. In the past you could only accomplish these things by making a great effort and after years of hard moral training. Now, you swallow two or three half-gramme tablets, and there you are. Anybody can be virtuous now. You can carry at least half your mortality about in a bottle. Christianity without tears—that's what *soma* is."

The Savage refutes Mond's philosophy: "'But I don't want comfort. I want God, I want poetry, I want real danger, I want freedom, I want goodness. I want sin.'" Denied the aspects of life which he regards most essential, John decides that he must escape from society. He retreats to a deserted lighthouse and there claims the right to rebel against society by punishing himself for his real and imagined sins. Even at the lighthouse, however, he is not safe. His odd actions draw a large crowd of curiosity seekers. John concludes that he can never find peace in this new world. One morning he is found hanging in the lighthouse with his feet revolving slowly from the north to the east and then back again—like a Hamlet who is but mad directionally.

Before his suicide John discovers that there is an enormous difference between the description of utopia and utopia in fact. He remembers the stories his mother told him about "that beautiful, beautiful Other Place, whose memory, as of a heaven, a paradise of goodness and loveliness, he still kept whole and intact, undefiled by contact with the reality of this real London, these actual civilized men and women." The Savage's comment underlines a central theme in *Brave New World.* While the fiction of a perfect world is interesting, one should be mindful of reaching that utopia—of the very concept of progress; for, once in the "ideal" commonwealth, the individual may find a wide disparity between his dreams and reality. Utopianism, Huxley feels, "runs the risk of becoming ruthless, of liquidating the people it happens to find inconvenient now for the sake of the people who are going, hypothetically, to be so much better and happier and more intelligent in the year 2000."[3] One should live for the present—the "here and now" Huxley calls it in *Island*—rather than aiming one's sights toward some future perfect that progress will provide. John's discovery that the Other Place must censor art, restrain individuality, do away with love, and prohibit innovation in order to maintain stability reminds him that the myth and the reality of utopia are very different indeed.

---

3. From a letter to Julian Huxley in *Letters of Aldous Huxley,* ed. Grover Smith (New York: Harper and Row, 1969), p. 483.

The Rise of Mass Man

Laurence Brander

Huxley's preoccupation with and concern about the increasing prosperity and numbers of the proletariat found expression in *Brave New World*, writes Laurence Brander. Huxley felt the masses had grown more menacing with population increases, according to Brander, and he wrote the novel at a time when it seemed mankind could not recover from the problems of war, depression, and explosive technological progress. Brander has also written books on George Orwell, E.M. Forster, and W. Somerset Maugham.

Brave New World is in great contrast with Huxley's earlier novels, which rely on characters, mood and atmosphere, qualities which are achieved by subtle and sensitive writing. *Brave New World*, a nightmare scientific future for Britain, requires the plain, quiet prose of scientific exposition. All the more because in this technicoloured technological future our values are turned upside down and the narrator must make it easy for us to suspend disbelief. Affection and loyalty are unnecessary, beauty is a synthetic product, truth is arranged in a test tube, hope is supplied in a pill, which by its action annihilates identity. Huxley supposed his nightmare to be thousands of years away but later on, he wondered whether parts of it were not alarmingly near. He returned to his Utopia twice, in a Foreword in 1946 and in *Brave New World Revisited* in 1958. The skills involved in conditioning humanity continued to interest him; for his Utopia is a reaction to the growth of Mass Man, and the masses have grown more menacing year by year.

In an essay on 'Revolutions' he noted two phases: 'The industrials of last century were living at the time of the population's most rapid increase. There was an endless supply of slaves. They could afford to be extravagant. . . Wage-slaves were worked to death at high speed; but there were always new ones coming in to take their places, fairly begging the capitalists to work *them* to death too.' While already in the nineteen-twenties, Huxley says: 'In the most fully industrialised countries the Proletariat is no longer abject; it is prosperous, its way of life approximates to that of the bourgeoisie. No longer the victims, it is actually, in some places, coming to be the victimiser.'. . .

THE UTOPIAN TRADITION

As so often in the Huxley oeuvre, a subject much on his mind appears in his fiction as well as in his essays. The rise of Mass Man impelled him to science fiction and the result is still his most popular novel. He uses a formula which George Orwell adopted in *1984*, horror supported by a strong sex theme. Huxley took his horrors gaily; Orwell took them savagely. Both books are dismal developments of one of the Utopian traditions in English writing. The other tradition is the optimistic idealism in More's *Utopia* (1516), right through to Morris's *News from Nowhere* (1890), and Wells's *Modern Utopia* (1905). The satirical tradition develops from Swift's *Gulliver's Travels* (1726) to Butler's *Erewhon* (1872), and the same vigorous, satirical inventiveness is seen in *Brave New World* and *1984*. Each strain is critical and corrective.

In More, the best kind of human being, his Syphogrants, Wells's *Samurai*, would lead the rest towards more agreeable ways of living and there would be a steady evolution towards heaven on earth. More's *Utopia*, like all classics, is contemporary. We can still profit by listening to him. He is against the waste of working hours in manufacturing unnecessary rubbish; he is all for a kind of Christian communism to abate our island acquisitiveness; he notes that men are much better ruled by men of other nations. These sixteenth-century suggestions would much improve our prospects. Morris is romantic, less practical, which is odd in a man who used his hands more than More ever did. *News from Nowhere* takes us back to a dream Thames valley agricultural heaven in which everyone is happily at work, doing what he likes and therefore never idle, always diligent. From More to Morris our Utopians are against our English idleness. The atmosphere of Morris is the endearing atmosphere of the youth of the world, when everyone was so sophisticated that society was gay and easy. We are reminded that all our classical Utopias are agricultural heavens in which there is no population problem but plenty of room for everyone. Everyone is well clothed and well fed. Most important of all, it is taken for granted that everyone is sane. The mental diseases which are universal among the human species and which have always prevented our English communities from becoming a society, have all disappeared.

It is our modern preoccupation with social and political insanity which colours our modern Utopias, and makes *Brave New World* and *1984* so different even from the satirical Utopias which went before. It is ironic that when at last all men could be properly housed, clothed and fed, we are teetering on the edge of an almost universal destruction and conduct our affairs with apparently irremediable lunacy. It may be that our knowledge explosion, with its shattering technical progress, has knocked us off balance and when we recover we shall succeed in imposing control. It may be that the natural balance in human affairs requires that great advances imply equally great dangers. When Huxley and Orwell wrote their Utopias, western man was struggling in the deepest trough of his despair. It seemed that the mental and spiritual life of mankind was so distorted that it could never recover. It was difficult in those decades to see any hope for the human race and their visions give typical pictures of our despair.

OVERPOPULATION

In *Brave New World* Huxley is facing particularly the fear of overpopulation, which since then has become a nightmare. In 'The Double Crisis', an essay published in *Themes and Variations* (1950), he says: 'The human race is passing through a time of crisis, and that crisis exists, so to speak, on two levels—an upper level of political and economic crisis and a lower level of demographic and ecological crisis.' He goes on to argue that the one affects the other and offers sensible solutions. It is a very living problem and has been so for a long time. Even in the twenties, the press of people on the earth was noticeable and it was apparent that they were forming a mass. What passes for education had made them so and as early as 1915 Wilfrid Trotter had demonstrated the necessity for new techniques of mass management in his *Conduct of the Herd in Peace and War*. The most eloquent analysis of the situation was offered by Ortega y Gasset in his *Revolt of the Masses* (1930). 'Europe', he says in his opening sentences, 'is suffering from the greatest crisis that can afflict peoples, nations and civilisation.' He was not thinking of the coming war in Spain or the still more dreadful conflict which was to unsettle the world. He was thinking of population. 'Towns are full of people, houses full of tenants, hotels full of guests, trains full of travellers, cafés full of customers, parks full of promenaders, consulting-rooms of famous doctors full of patients, theatres full of spectators, and beaches full of bathers. What previously was, in general, no problem, now begins to be an every day one, namely, to find room.'

Huxley and Orwell face the problem of ruling these masses. They look at what we have made of our English democracy and substitute for that insanity a satirical insanity much more odious. Orwell produced a sick man's nightmare of sadism based on his observations of European totalitarianisms. Huxley wrote out of his scientific background and mass-produced his population in the fashion long popular in science fiction, growing them in bottles and conditioning them from birth in all the ways proposed by psychologists. Both heredity and environment were absolutely determined. These bottle products were released from moral tensions because they were so conditioned that none of their actions had moral consequences. They could always escape from reality very easily by the use of the standard drug, soma, which was a great improvement on alcohol or anything else known because it produced no unpleasant reactions and was benignly addictive. The people were always in a state of euphoria because the human spirit had been prisoned and confined in a perfectly conditioned healthy cadaver. 'And that', put in the Director sententiously, 'that is the seat of happiness and virtue—liking what you've *got* to do. All conditioning aims at that: making people like their inescapable social destiny.'

The old trouble in human societies, that some are more equal than others, has been resolved. The population problem has been resolved. People are manufactured as they are needed, a few Alpha Plus specimens, hundreds of Epsilons. It is fascinating, because, as in all these satires, it is a twist of known data, with the creative spirit working at white heat pursuing every absurdity the original twist suggests. The normal is the extravagant and outrageous and once the reader has been conditioned to accept this inverted normalcy, opposition is introduced to make the tale. Accidents happen when the bottles are in production and that gives us two high intelligence characters who are misfits. A little alcohol accidently splashed into the bottle, perhaps. The story wants something more, so the Savage is introduced. He was born viviparously, out of a careless Beta Minus who had gone with an Alpha Plus male on a trip to the native reservation, one of the settlements of old type human beings still in existence. A pregnant Beta Minus could not possibly be brought back to England, so she stays to give birth to a son and supports him by prostitution. He is a young man when we meet him, with a strong individuality stimulated by reading Shakespeare; just the opposition the story requires, a romantic idealist in a controlled society.

A SCIENTIFICALLY MANUFACTURED AND CONTROLLED SOCIETY

The purpose of the book is to give us a full picture of a society scientifically manufactured and controlled and the story is a means to that end. If any reader flags, he will be sexually titillated. Orwell used the same device. Huxley is creating a country according to the prophet Ford, who developed mass production. 'Standard men and women in uniform batches.' Electric shocks when babies crawl towards pretty flowers or pretty pictures; 'saved from books and botany all their lives.' Erotic play in children encouraged; they will be young for all the sixty years of their lives and enormously potent, and in this will lie their natural happiness. The women will never conceive and everyone can and should be completely promiscuous. It would be unnatural and unsocial to go steady. There are no families and there is no mother love. What we call friendship develops only between the misfits. Average citizens lived under the influence of soma all their lives and therefore without individuality or integrity. In 1932 Huxley thought this was a remote nightmare but already in 1946 he confessed that his brave new world was coming quicker than he had expected. The core of the book is the argument on happiness between the Controller and the Savage. They argue like a couple of Oxford dons on the name and nature of happiness in society. The Savage reveals a power in dialectic for which his past life, one would have thought, had hardly prepared him. Huxley is right. It would have been better if the Savage had had another background, something worth preferring. As it is, he has to choose between the squalor of the Reservation and the spiritless shallow happiness of the world according to Ford. He tried to find another alternative. He sought solitude and silence in a disused lighthouse on the south coast. Despite his continued study of Shakespeare he could not get away from thoughts of Lenina. Huxley later confessed in *Texts and Pretexts* a small slip there: 'I wanted this person to be a platonic lover; but, reading through the plays, I realized to my dismay that platonic love is not a subject with which Shakespeare ever deals.' The Savage flagellates himself to subdue the flesh. He is observed. All the resources of mass communication go into operation and very soon hordes of the public descend upon him. Among them is Lenina, the fair temptress. The Savage makes the escape of the creature that is hurt too much; he kills himself.

THE PARABLE OF THE INDIVIDUAL

It is the parable of the individual in the mass community. We live in the age of the mass. The politicians, the salesmen, the entertainers, all who batten on the mass exacerbate the instincts which sway human beings as a mass. The decent individual is carried along, still protesting but more than ever lost. In our timid totalitarianism the individual is bruised and frustrated by forces as impersonal as nature herself. In *Brave New World* and *1984* the implacable scrutiny of the state is directed on them all the time. The 'proles' are easily controlled; it is the individualistic party member who can cause trouble, the misfit Bernard and [*1984*'s] pitiful Winston. With individuals so marked, dynamic progress becomes impossible and both these books present us with the static state. As such states have always crashed, Huxley and Orwell are at pains to explain how the rulers secured stability. . . .

PROPHECIES QUICKLY FULFILLED

In 1958, Huxley returned to his Utopian theme in *Brave New World Revisited* . . . to express his alarm at the speed at which his prophecies in *Brave New World* were being fulfilled. He had thought that 'the completely organized society, the scientific caste system, the abolition of free will by methodical conditioning, the servitude made acceptable by regular doses of chemically-induced happiness, the orthodoxies drummed in by nightly courses of sleep-teaching—these things were coming all right, but not in my time, not even in the time of my grandchildren.' Our gruesome planet was radically different from the gruesome brave new world. 'Ours was a nightmare of too little order; theirs, in the seventh century A.F. of too much.' But now, in 1958: 'I feel a great deal less optimistic than I did when I was writing *Brave New World.*' He sees that 'the nightmare of total organization has emerged from the safe, remote future and is now awaiting us, just around the next corner.' It follows inexorably from having so many people.

He agrees that 'for a long time to come we shall remain a viviparous species breeding at random' and it follows that control must be post-natal; but his book is about the very adequate control now available to rulers and tycoons. It has been found that the best way with men, as with animals, is to dangle rewards in front of them and to give enough to ensure that they go on reacting to the reward system. Men are proving easily corruptible and the very concept of freedom is fading. Free men are being drowned in the Mass, which has been produced by the machines and the chemists. This, says Huxley in 1958, is the urgent problem of our age and all our thoughts about conquering space are irrelevant.

Brave New World Satirizes the American Present, Not the British Future

Peter Firchow

There's no point in satirizing the future, Huxley scholar Peter Firchow suggests; Huxley was not aiming his barbs at the future of his compatriots in England so much as at the then-current state of affairs in the United States. Firchow notes that Huxley was especially impressed (not especially positively) by Los Angeles, with its hectic activity, ubiquitous advertising, and, as Firchow puts it, "hardly any trace of intellectual life or purpose."

Huxley almost certainly never intended *Brave New World* to be a satire of the future. For what, after all, is the good of satirizing the future? The only meaningful future is actually, as he observed in an essay published a year earlier, the future which already exists in the present. "O brave new world," let us remember, is what Miranda exclaims when she sees for the first time the as yet unredeemed inhabitants of the *old* world, an irony of which Huxley is fully aware. The present is what matters most in *Brave New World*, as it does in any good Utopia; and Huxley only uses the lens of future time (as preceding satirists had often resorted to geographical or past remoteness) in order to discover better the latent diseases of the here and now.[1] . . .

1. Another example of an anti-Utopia which uses a projection into the future to satirize the present is the Russian novelist Zamiatin's *We*. This work is occasionally mentioned as an influence on *Brave New World*, but Zamiatin's connection with *1984* seems more immediate.

In quite another, and rather more trivial, sense, *Brave New World* is also an attack on the present's conception of the future. Specifically, it is a parody of H.G. Wells's optimistic fantasy of the future, *Men Like Gods*. This is confirmed by Huxley in a letter

(continued on next page)

Excerpted from Peter Firchow, *Aldous Huxley: Satirist and Novelist* (Minneapolis: University of Minnesota Press, 1972). Copyright © 1972 by Peter Firchow. Reprinted by permission of the author.

Los Angeles: "Joy City"

In 1926 Huxley made a trip around the world, traveling eastward and stopping primarily in India, Burma, Malaya, and the United States, paying his bills by writing up his experiences for British and American papers. Later in the same year he collected these fragments and joined them together in *Jesting Pilate*, a fascinating travelogue of a man in search of the truth but too pressed to stay for a definite answer—but not too pressed to await and formulate provisional ones, such as the "truth" (which was later to become a massive lie for the author of *Island*) that the ways of the East were not noticeably superior to those of Europe, or the "truth" that Western culture in its westernmost or Californian manifestations boded ill for the future of mankind.

In a special section of *Jesting Pilate* entitled "Los Angeles. A Rhapsody," Huxley records his impressions of the City of Dreadful Joy, or more briefly, the Joy City, with devastating irony. Los Angeles, as Huxley perceives it, is a city in which everybody is happy but no one is quite sure why, where there is hectic activity on all sides, with people rushing to and fro in their automobiles, bombarded by advertising and enticed by entertainment of every sort, from religious to alcoholic, but where there is hardly any trace of intellectual life or purpose. Here man, as in the brave new world, is created for the good time, not the good time for man, with the inescapable consequence that his soul and body become standardized. The women, for example, are "plumply ravishing" and give promise (as do their equivalents in the newer world) of an Eliotesque "pneumatic bliss"—"but of not much else, to judge by their faces. So curiously uniform, unindividual and blank" (*Jesting Pilate*, page 266). For Huxley, it is plain, there is no need to travel into the future to find the brave new world; it already exists, only too palpably, in the American Joy City, where the declaration of dependence begins and ends with the single-minded pursuit of happiness.

dated May 18, 1931: "I am writing a novel about the future—on the horror of the Wellsian Utopia and a revolt against it" (*Letters of Aldous Huxley*, London, 1969, p. 348). In *Private History* (London, 1960), p. 154, Derek Patmore relates how Wells reacted to this revolt: "Ever an ardent socialist, he was certain that social progress would cure the evils that men were so easily prone to, and when we discussed the works of such writers as Aldous Huxley he said to me savagely: '*Brave New World* was a great disappointment to me. A writer of the standing of Aldous Huxley has no right to betray the future as he did in that book. When thinking about the future, people seem to overlook the logical progress in education, in architecture, and science.'"

Typically "American," too, is the rejection of everything old [in *Brave New World*]. "History," Mustapha Mond remarks, citing one of the prime commandments of Our Ford, "is bunk." And not just written history or old books—Shakespeare and the Bible which have to be locked away in a safe—but all old ideas and institutions are bunk. The very concept of age is bunk for those who live modern in the soma generation. How horrified the orthodox Fordians are by the unexpected appearance of a woman who reveals her actual age in wrinkles, sagging breasts, and flabby flesh! How disgusted even that woman herself is by her own condition, exiled though she has been from earthly paradise for more than two decades!

No Choice but to Be Young

In the new world, youth is not merely skin-deep. It penetrates far into the interior of the Fordian psyche, so far in fact that the lower orders have no choice but to be young. Heredity and conditioning will not permit them to think or act otherwise than in an infantile fashion. Only the Alphas, the managerial elite of the Fordian state, "do not *have* to be infantile in their emotional behavior." This, however, does not mean that they are freed from the obligation of maintaining "a proper standard of infantile decorum," though to be sure a few Alphas like Bernard Marx or Helmholtz Watson do occasionally behave in indecorous adult ways. But their example can have no permanent effect, for the very simple reason that adults are removed at once from the society.

The only adults who are permitted to influence the Fordian state are the twelve so-called World Controllers, who function as a tiny priest class governing a vast population of blissfully ignorant babies. To judge by the example of Mustapha Mond, however, the World Controllers are a very sober and benevolent group who selflessly devote themselves to the welfare of their charges. Mond himself, as a former physicist of considerable promise, would have been happier pursuing his scientific researches undisturbed, but instead he chose the harder and less rewarding task of government. It is on his shoulders, and on those of his eleven peers, that the ultimate responsibility for the operation of the Fordian state rests.

The Church of Rome

Though there is no religion in the new world beyond the materialistically oriented orgy-porgy services—sustained youth, as Mond observes to the Savage, allows one to be independent of God—the World Controllers seem fairly clearly to be modeled on the pope and cardinals of the Church of Rome. Like these, Mond is a father to his "children," guarding them from the burden and temptations of excessive knowledge and filling their lives with time-consuming pomp and circumstance. The Fordian state—even phrases like "Our Ford" or "Ford's in his flivver" imply it—resembles nothing so much as a secular theocracy.

That Huxley is fully conscious of this dimension of his satirical parable is implicit in the extended dialogue between Mond and the Savage which occupies all of chapter 17. This chapter is a revision of the Grand Inquisitor episode in Dostoevsky's *Brothers Karamazov*, with the roles of the Inquisitor and Christ reversed. Here it is the Christ-Savage who is indignant at the behavior of the Inquisitor-Controller and his presumption that man can live by soma alone. To be sure, unlike Dostoevsky's Christ, Huxley's Controller does not maintain absolute silence in the face of his interlocutor's verbal onslaught, but he does the next best thing by seeking to overcome the Savage's objections through sweet reasonableness. Of course, like Christ he can afford to be tolerant, for he holds the supreme power in his hands: he rules over the godless utopia whose coming the Grand Inquisitor had foretold. That utopia exists—unlike Christ's heaven—not for the chosen few, who are in any event strong enough to help themselves, but for the masses of the weak and spineless, who don't know what to do with Christ's gift of freedom and who are only too pleased to rid themselves of the "terrible burden of that gift" in exchange for "being able to become a herd once again." The historical development of the Fordian world, as related by Mond, conforms strikingly to the pattern predicted by the Grand Inquisitor: "Oh, ages are yet to come of the confusion of free thought, of their science and cannibalism. For having begun to build their tower of Babel without us, they will end, of course with cannibalism. But then the beast will crawl to us and lick our feet and spatter them with tears of blood. . . . But then, and only then, the reign of peace and happiness will come for men. Thou art proud of Thine elect, but Thou hast only the elect, while we give rest to all. . . . With us all will be happy and will no more rebel nor destroy one another as under Thy freedom. Oh, we shall persuade them that they will only become free when they renounce their freedom to us and submit to us" (page 238).[2] In its essential outline, though not in its proportions and its technological details, the new world matches the Grand Inquisitor's vision: "And all will be happy, all the millions of creatures except for the hundred thousand who rule over them. For only we, we who guard the mystery, shall be unhappy. There will be thousands of millions of happy ones and a hundred thousand sufferers who have taken upon themselves the curse of the knowledge of good and evil (page 239)."

Against this enforced happiness, the Savage asserts the "right to be unhappy," the right to deformity, to disease and suffering of all kinds, the right to endure pain and to limit pleasure. To Mustapha Mond, as to the Grand Inquisitor, the desire for and the exercise of such a right seem the only evils of which they can conceive. In the end, as in Ivan Karamazov's tale, one or the other "right" must triumph, and the other vanish utterly. It must be either soul or stomach, the love of God or the love of man: there is no other alternative.

THE AMERICAN DREAM

In the United States, especially in its westernmost parts, Huxley found incarnated most of the dream of the Grand Inquisitor, found the love of stomach and of mass man running rampant, and recognized that what confronted him here was the future of mankind. At the very beginning of "The Outlook for American Culture: Some Reflections in a Machine Age," an essay published in 1927, Huxley warned his readers that "speculating on the American future, we are speculating on the future of civilized man." One of the most ominous portents of the American way of life, Huxley went on to say, was that it embraced a large class of people who "do not want to be cultured, are not interested in the higher life. For these people existence on the lower, animal levels is perfectly satisfactory. Given food, drink, the company of their fellows, sexual enjoyment, and plenty of noisy distractions from without, they are happy." Furthermore, in America and the rest of the technologically advanced world, "all the resources of science are applied in order that imbecility may flourish and vulgarity cover the whole earth." The resources are so applied because quantity rather than quality is profitable for the capitalists involved: "The higher the degree of standardization in popular literature and art, the greater the profit for the

2. Passages from *The Brothers Karamazov* are quoted from the New American Library edition, trans. Constance Garnett (New York, 1957).

manufacturer." All this mechanical and intellectual standard-ization, however, leads to the exaltation of the standardized man. It is this development which Huxley views with most con-cern: "This tendency to raise the ordinary, worldly man to the level of the extraordinary and disinterested one seems to me en-tirely deplorable. The next step will be to exalt him above the ex-traordinary man, who will be condemned and persecuted on principle because he is not ordinary—for not to be ordinary will be regarded as a crime. In this reversal of the old values I see a real danger, a menace to all desirable progress."[3]

It is this "next step" that has been taken in the Fordian (that is, American) world. For of all ideas, the idea of the extraordi-nary or individual can least be tolerated by the new world. Extraordinary or individual behavior is a punishable offense. That is why the father of John the Savage, a Director of Hatch-eries and Conditioning, hastens to assure Bernard that he had had "nothing emotional, nothing long-drawn" to do with the girl he had taken on a visit to a New Mexico Reservation; that is, the girl who was accidentally left behind and thus gave birth (another offense) to the Savage. This is also why he cen-sures Bernard for suspected individualism, for not conform-ing to the duty of all Alphas "to be infantile, even against their inclination." The Alpha must inhibit his illicit desires for adult behavior, must sacrifice his individuality for the sake of social solidarity and uniformity. But as the examples of Marx and Watson reveal, not all Alphas do so.

Consequently, in spite of all the attempts of technology and psychological conditioning to reduce man to an au-tomaton, some semblance of humanity and individuality still survives, even if only accidentally. In this respect, *Brave New World* is not entirely the deeply pessimistic novel it is usually considered to be; the hope for a continuation of hu-manity is not altogether extinguished. It is the same hope that Huxley offered to his contemporaries in an essay, "Fore-heads Villainous Low" (a title also derived from *The Tem-pest*), published a year before the novel, at a time when the gathering powers of fascism and economic depression in-clined the majority of thinking men either to despair or to desperate measures: "The new snobberies of stupidity and ignorance are now strong enough to wage war at least on equal terms with the old culture-snobbery. For still, an ab-

3. Aldous Huxley, "The Outlook for American Culture, Some Reflections in a Machine Age," *Harper's Magazine*, 155 (August 1927), 265–270.

surd anachronism, the dear old culture-snobbery bravely survives. Will it go down before its enemies? And, much more important, will the culture it so heroically and ridiculously stands up for, also go down? I hope, I even venture to think, it will not. There will always be a few people for whom the things of the mind are so vitally important that they will not, they simply cannot allow them to be overwhelmed" (*Music at Night*, pages 208–209).

Yet, though the new world has its quota of individual survivors, the atmosphere of their environment is so oppressive that it is nearly impossible for them to increase their awareness of themselves or each other. Bernard Marx has come to realize that he is distinct from the mass of other Alphas only because too much alcohol was accidentally added to his blood surrogate. Helmholtz Watson has arrived at a similar perception by the more natural but equally casual expedient of having been born too intelligent to accept his conditioning uncritically. The two become friends because they are aware of something in themselves that makes them different, but their awareness is stifled at every turn. Their surroundings offer them almost no opportunity to express themselves. Bernard struggles ineffectively to establish a human relationship with Lenina Crowne; Helmholtz Watson strives for the poetical formulation of something he as yet only remotely understands. But only when they come into contact with the Savage do they finally become aware of the means for an expression of themselves.

THE SAVAGE IS TEMPORARILY SANE

The Savage is an individual. Nevertheless, though he comes from a society which is in its externals totally different from that of the Fordian world, he is, like Bernard, an individual merely by accident. Because of his racial distinctness (and because of what is considered the immorality of his mother), he is not accepted by the Indian society in which he grows up. Yet, again like Bernard, he desperately wants to be a part of this society, wants to belong; in other words, he has been conditioned, to use a word Huxley employs in his later preface, to the "insane" behavior of a "religion that is half fertility cult and half *Penitente* ferocity."[4] He does eventually manage, however, to break partly free from the vicious circle of his conditioning through the liberating influence of Shakespeare and the shock

4. The 1946 preface to the novel reprinted in the *Collected Works Edition*, p. viii.

of his sudden encounter with the "lunacy" (to quote again from the same preface) of the new world. For the brief period before his fated relapse into insane *Penitente*-ism and his subsequent suicide, John is a sane, human individual.

As such, he rejects the lunacy of the new world and refuses to accept as an ideal a happiness bought at the expense of a total abandonment of humanity. He wants to feel *as* an individual *for* an individual, not as automaton for an automaton, as in the orgy-porgian Solidarity Services. That is why he persists, in face of the only too self-evident facts, in conceiving of Lenina as an individual. He is not content with her merely as a "pneumatic" object for sexual satisfaction; he must love her as a human being or not at all. To love her as a human being, however, as he gradually comes to realize, is impossible. To love her not at all is not easy. Alone in his tower, haunted by the sensual images of her body, he once more reverts to his former *Penitente* conditioning. The ingrained idea of sin will not permit him to think of sex as a normal human activity. For him it is evil and must be punished: first by self-flagellation, later by suicide. He is a male Miranda who, convinced he has found his Ferdinand, discovers to his horror that beneath the real morocco surrogate clothing lurks none other than Caliban. In the end, exiled from the vile old world and disgusted by the brave new one, he has no place to go but into the desert.[5] Even there, however, he cannot escape the power of Prospero-Mustapha's gray magic or the force of his own primitive conditioning. The noble savage, the World Controller's "experiment" finally demonstrates, can only exist where there are opportunities to be both noble and savage. And that is not Ford's world, where one can never be man or beast, but only machine.

The problem posed by the intrusion of the Savage is that in neither society—the insane Indian or the lunatic Fordian—is there any provision for the human individual. Both societies have abolished individuality in order to become either subhumanly bestial or subhumanly mechanical. Both have paid far too high a price for social stability; and both, despite this stability, are consequently inferior to the unstable, unjust, unhappy, but still relatively human society of early twentieth-century Europe.

In the series of portraits of this twentieth-century society which Huxley satirically sketched in his earlier novels, the

5. Is there some autobiographical significance in Huxley's choice of a tower not far from Godalming—his own birthplace—for the Savage to commit suicide in?

fatal flaw was always the isolation of the individual. He was alone, trapped in his own conception of reality. This is not the case with the society of the brave new world, or, to a lesser degree, with that of the Indian *Penitentes*. In these societies the individual is solidly integrated, to the point of becoming an almost indistinguishable part of the whole. Too solidly, too indistinguishably—that is what is wrong with them. The price of social solidarity is the loss of individual existence. This is the paradox at the very heart of the novel: to be individual is to be isolated and unhappy; to be integrated is to be "happy," but happy in an inhuman fashion. It is the happiness, in the words of one of Huxley's early poems, of a "great goggling fish," or that, as Mustapha Mond remarks, of being confined inside a bottle whose walls exclude any reality and any awareness but that which is allowed to filter through.

Huxley later came to consider the exclusion of no suitable alternative to piscine bliss or wretched individuality to be an artistic fault of the novel. In his view, *Brave New World* should have proposed another possibility, that of "sanity.". . .

Thirty years after *Brave New World*, Huxley fictionalized this third possibility at length and in detail in *Island*. But even in *Brave New World* itself some such possibility is already vaguely adumbrated in the happy-unhappy islands to which Bernard and Helmholtz are finally exiled.

The central problem of *Brave New World* could also be phrased in another way. The inhabitants of the Fordian state are aware (insomuch as they are aware of anything) of a reality which is totally "happy"; the inhabitants of the Indian Reservation (including, for the most part, the Savage), on the other hand, are aware only of a sinister, "unhappy" reality. In neither society is there an awareness of the whole truth, that is of all realities, sinister, "happy," and the multitude of intervening shadings; in fact, both are posited on a negation of this whole truth. Both societies, consequently—and the "individuals" they comprise—are imprisoned in their preconceptions of reality and are essentially unaware. But unawareness of the whole truth, as the novels up to and including *Point Counter Point* indicated, leads either to individual isolation or to the animality of the Complete Man; it does not lead to an integration commensurate with true humanity. And it is precisely because *Brave New World*, when measured against such a standard, is found sorely wanting that it is a bitterly destructive satire.

Big Nanny Is Watching

Philip Yancey

"Big Brother Is Watching" is a familiar warning from George Orwell's anti-utopian novel, *1984*. While the horrors of *1984* did not arrive—at least, not on time— the more subtle dangers of *Brave New World* still threaten, writes Philip Yancey, an editor at large for *Christianity Today*. Where Orwell's fantasy world re- lied on pain to force compliance, Huxley's seduced with pleasure; his "Big Nanny" promises comfort and safety. Yancey ventures a guess about the characteris- tics of an updated brave new world, and finds we are appallingly close to achieving it.

Polish playwright Janusz Glowacki recalls visiting a "This Is America" exhibit in Warsaw during the darkest days of Stalinism. While listening to a decadent boogie-woogie soundtrack, he gravely filed past displays of loud ties, gaudy billboards, KKK crosses, and even insects from Colorado that were supposedly dropped from planes at night to devour socialists' potatoes. "The exhibition was meant to evoke hor- ror, disgust, and hatred," he says. "It had, however, the op- posite effect. Thousands of Varsovians, dressed in their hol- iday best, waited every day in lines as long as those to see Lenin's Tomb and in solemn silence looked at the display, listened respectfully to the boogie-woogie, wanting in this way, at least, to manifest their blind and hopeless love for the United States."

Now, thanks to the astonishing changes in Europe, Poles and even Russians can freely design their own loud ties and gaudy billboards and compose their own boogie-woogie. Against all odds, Western culture has triumphed, with very few shots being fired. With the U.S. no longer defining its identity in opposition to communism, what lies ahead?

Author Neil Postman suggests that though we seem to have escaped George Orwell's *1984*, we are still in peril from

Reprinted from Philip Yancey, "Big Nanny Is Watching You," *Christianity Today*, De- cember 16, 1991, by permission of *Christianity Today*.

Aldous Huxley's *Brave New World*. Those two books actually present quite different visions of the future—the difference between Big Brother and Big Nanny.

Orwell warned against an external enemy that relies on violence and propaganda to impose its will. In contrast, Huxley warned against a more subtle enemy from within. People will gladly trade away their freedom and autonomy for a technology that promises comfort, safety, and amusement, he predicted. Orwell's villains used a pain machine to enforce their decrees; Huxley's villains relied on pleasure. Orwell's regime banned books; in Huxley's fantasy, books are plentiful but no one wants to read one.

UPDATING A GENTLE NIGHTMARE

Since 1984 has come and gone, perhaps it is time to update Huxley's gentle nightmare. What would a "Brave New Society" look like?

1. *A Brave New Society repairs the defects in human personality.* Neurophysiologist José M. R. Delgado made a splash a few years back when he brought a charging bull to a dead stop by pressing a button on a radio transmitter. (He had implanted an electrode in the bull's brain.) The title of his book describing this and other experiments says it well: *Physical Control of the Mind: Toward a Psychocivilized Society.*

Open the spigot of government funds, say the behavioral scientists, and we will identify the physiological bases of addictions or sexual and personality disorders. Then we can repair them through drugs or surgery.

Admittedly, a defect-free society would forfeit potentially valuable contributions from deviants. Would Beethoven, Schubert, and Brahms have bothered with their music if their personality disorders had been repaired? We might have lost Jerome's Vulgate translation that served the church for 1,000 years (he worked on it as a means of sublimating sexual desire), and Augustine might have watered down his *Confessions.* But just think how Abraham Lincoln—who rarely smiled, struggled with depression, and was married to a probable psychopath—might have been improved!

2. *A Brave New Society simplifies morality.* The new society dispenses with such notions as absolute truth and "inalienable rights." Only two principles matter: kindness and tolerance.

Politically correct thinking, based on kindness and tolerance, will insist on certain cultural adjustments. *Huckleberry*

Finn and the Brothers Grimm will need reworking. Anti-Semitic passages in Shakespeare must be excised. Can a Politically Correct Bible be far behind? (Zacchaeus was, after all, not "short," but "vertically challenged.")

3. *A Brave New Society solves problems through technology.* C. S. Lewis wrote, "For the wise men of old, the cardinal problem of human life was how to conform the soul to objective reality, and the solution was wisdom, self-discipline, and virtue. For the modern mind, the cardinal problem is how to subdue reality to the wishes of man, and the solution is a technique."

We apply the criteria "developed, less-developed, under-developed" to Brave New Societies, avoiding such value-laden words as *just, moral, good.* Sad-eyed prophets like Solzhenitsyn used to argue that the suffering East could teach spiritual values to the materialistic West. I haven't heard that argument lately; the East is too busy trying to catch up to the economic standards of the West.

Africa and parts of Asia seem beyond our technological

THE CATERWAULING OF POPULAR MUSIC

Bemoaning the quality of music made for a mass audience, Huxley says there may not be a cure for such a debasement of art, but offers a hint about how to teach young people to tell beauty from ugliness.

What has happened in the realm of literature has happened also in that of popular music. But here the invention of talking machines rather than primary education has created a big audience of listeners. . . . Listening matter is needed for this huge audience: it is manufactured, and inevitably it is of very poor quality. But in the case of popular music things are complicated by aesthetic matters. For the last 130 years musicians have greatly developed the technical means used to express their feelings. Beethoven created a whole repertoire of technical means to express the passions—means unknown to even his brilliant predecessors. The enrichment of musical technique progressed throughout the nineteenth century. Berlioz, Wagner, Verdi, the Russians, Debussy—all contributed new means of expression to the common stock. Naturally the feelings these composers aimed to express did not always have the purity and nobility that characterize Beethoven's. Wagner, especially, gave music the power to express—and with great capacity to fix. They will have their place in the Brave New Society, too: we'll watch two-minute reports on the devastation, sandwiched in-between the sports and weather.

4. *A Brave New Society elevates entertainment above all other values.* George Orwell feared a Big Brother whose projected image would intrude in every home. The screens are in place now, but we choose the images we want, and the bottom line is entertainment.

American families watch television five to seven hours a day, demonstrating an obsession with entertainment unmatched in history. Naturally, the medium affects the message. Watch *Sesame Street* for three minutes and you'll see what education looks like when forced through an entertainment grid. Or, compare the successful televangelist programs with the average local church service. Television is not the only measure of how much we value entertainment. Consider that a good baseball pitcher earns twice as much for nine innings' work as a high-school physics teacher earns in a year.

power of artistic persuasion—things that are fundamentally despicable. Popular composers have learned their craft from the great artists. Thanks to Beethoven, Berlioz, Wagner, Rimski-Korsakov and Debussy, they are now in a position to express with gripping power the basest emotions—the most abject sentimentality, the most animal sexuality and the most frenetic collective joy. . . .

The disease is not completely curable, but I believe it can be mitigated, firstly through education. We pay too little attention to the development of taste and a critical faculty; or if we try to develop them, we always choose remote, outdated examples. If I had to teach young people the art of telling beauty from ugliness, the real from the imitation, I would try to choose my examples from the contemporary world. I would focus their critical faculties on politicians' speeches and on advertising. I would get them to hear the differences in quality between a piece of jazz and one of Beethoven's late quartets. I would get them to read some detective story, and then *Crime and Punishment* or *The Possessed.*

Aldous Huxley, "A Defence of the Intellect," speech given at the International Institute of Intellectual Co-operation's meeting on the future of the European mind, October 16–18, 1933, in Paris, France. Reprinted in the *Unesco Courier*, December 1993.

A Famous Song

How close are we to achieving the Brave New Society? A recent visit to the British Museum Library gave me pause. One room displays original letters and manuscript pages from great authors, arranged chronologically. I spent several hours there, proceeding from Shakespeare to Jane Austen to Virginia Woolf. Finally I reached the most recent manuscript collection. There, displayed in a formal wooden case with gold-leaf lettering, was the scrawled original of one of the most famous songs of this half-century: "Oh yeah, oh yeah, I wanna hold your hand." The poet had captured the spirit of the age precisely.

Brave New World, Sixty Years Later

John Clute

The twentieth century, writes John Clute, editor of *The Encyclopedia of Science Fiction,* has been the century of change, and the fear is that the change will stop at the wrong time and lock us into a nightmare. This fear of fixity is the real nightmare at the heart of *Brave New World,* he asserts. When Huxley wrote of a world locked into a single vision of artificial happiness, he produced an act of prophecy that is still powerful today.

Towards the end of the 1950s, his creative energies thinned out by age, ill-health and too many years in southern California, Aldous Huxley wrote a series of articles about the future for *Newsday.* In a tone of wearied candour, he outlined for his American audience the issues that seemed urgent at the time: overpopulation; the excessive organisation of society; propaganda; the chemistry of brainwashing; and so forth. Later, he revised these pieces into a book that he called *Brave New World Revisited* (1958).

This, precisely, it was not. *Brave New World* (1932) was an act of prophecy; its successor was a set of predictions. The first could not be falsified by a failure of world history to march according to its vision, and it remains subversively alive at the end of the century to which it gave a dream-shape. The second, which has been proved wrong in a dozen ways in accordance with the fate of all books of futurology, is just as dead as any work of predictive non-fiction by H G Wells.

In 1958, Huxley (who was born in 1894) understood *Brave New World* as a work that had predicted "the completely organised society, the scientific caste system, the abolition of free will by methodical conditioning, the servi-

tude made acceptable by regular doses of chemically induced happiness, the orthodoxies drummed in by nightly
courses of sleep-teaching".

Its only real flaw as futurology, beyond its failure to antic-
ipate the A-bomb, he wrote, lay in placing several centuries
hence the total victory of Technos through chemistry. He
then explained, in fatally erring detail, how this victory was
in fact upon us.

In 1993, other victories have superseded the futurama
horror imagined in 1958. Overpopulation has not led to icy
fixities of control, but to chaos: chemistry (and electronics)
do not marshal our days at the behest of Secret Masters, but
do give us chances to opt out into nirvana, into a seeming infinity of solipsisms. We have become street-wise to dystopia;
we inhabit a world of plethora and desecration that neither
Huxley nor any other futurologist half a century back could
have begun to wish on us. His wisdom lies elsewhere.

It has been estimated that the term "science fiction" appears fewer than a dozen times in the voluminous published

---

BAD CONTEMPORARY LITERATURE

*Huxley may have written a work that can be classified as
science fiction, but he worked hard to avoid the vulgarity of
"popular art." In this excerpt from a speech given a few months
after the publication of* Brave New World, *he bemoaned the pro-
liferation of inferior literature.*

Our times are anti-intellectualist; they are also vulgar. The contemporary lifestyle is frankly disgusting. . . . The quite specific
vulgarity of our era shows itself in the quite specific vulgarity of
our popular art, which is also the cause of it. As nearly always
happens, the movement is circular and vicious. What are the
causes of this vulgarity? They are partly economic and demographic, partly intellectual and aesthetic. Industrial development
and the development of virgin territory in the New World have
led to a sudden expansion of Europe's population, which has
more than doubled in one century. Next comes primary education for all. An enormous potential readership has been created,
for whom entrepreneurs have set up a new industry—the reading matter industry. Now this reading matter could only be and
will only be of very poor quality. Why? It is a matter of arith-
metic. The number of writers with artistic talent is always very
limited. So it follows that at any time the bulk of contemporary
literature has always been bad. Now the amount of literature

work of Aldous Huxley; but *Brave New World* remains a central work of that genre. The dominance of American SF from about 1925 to about 1975, with its technophilia [love of technology], its booster exuberance and its constant gatecrashing thrust into the future, has tended to conceal the true science fiction impulse. That is by no means consolatory. Wells, Huxley, Orwell, Philip K Dick and a dozen significant figures now writing have all used the devices of SF to host, and to grapple with, the nightmare of history during a century haunted by what might be called a radical of transformation.

The 20th century, in other words, is genuinely different. It is the century of change and of nightmares about the end of change. The profound impulse of science fiction is to gain perspectives on the quicksand; the profoundest fear of most serious writers of science fiction is that somehow the world will suddenly stop shifting at the wrong moment, locking us into a malign stasis.

The great dystopias of the 20th century are nightmares of tetanus. "If you want to imagine the future," said Orwell in

produced annually has grown faster than the population. There are twice as many of us today as there were at the beginning of the nineteenth century. But the number of printed words we consume each year is at least fifty—if not a hundred—times greater than the number consumed by our great-grandparents. Hence it follows that the percentage of bad literature in the total must be higher than ever. Europeans have got into the habit of reading all the time. It is a vice, like smoking cigarettes—or rather, perhaps, like smoking opium or taking to cocaine; for this literature, which is almost all bad, is a mental substitute for narcotic and hallucinatory drugs. Europe is being fed—stuffed, one might say—with tenth-rate literature.

This is completely new. In the past, people were only familiar directly or indirectly with a few books, but they were of very high quality. English people, for instance, until quite recently grew up with the Bible and Bunyan's *Pilgrim's Progress,* both of unmatched purity and nobility of style. Nowadays, they grow up with the *Daily Express,* magazines and detective stories. Universal education has had the lamentable result that instead of occasionally reading masterpieces people continually read rubbish.

Aldous Huxley, "A Defence of the Intellect," speech given at the International Institute of Intellectual Co-operation's meeting on the future of the European mind, October 16–18, 1933, in Paris, France. Reprinted in the *Unesco Courier,* December 1993.

Nineteen Eighty Four (1949), "Imagine a boot stamping on a human face for ever." "So it goes," says Kurt Vonnegut.

The terror at the heart of *Brave New World* is not the feelies, not babies in bottles, but fixity. The novel closes with the suicide of Mr Savage, the only character capable of reflecting our humane nostalgia for rounded human beings alive in a supple world. At the end, we can only see his feet:

> Slowly, very slowly, like two unhurried compass needles, the feet turned towards the right; north, north-east, east, south-east, south, south-south west; then paused, and after a few seconds, turned as unhurriedly towards the left, south-south-west, south, south-east, east.

Huxley's second great nightmare, *Ape and Essence* (1948), is in many ways a lesser book than its predecessor, though far more explicitly savage about human nature and history. It is the lesser creation, in part because its structure never gels.

There is a prologue in 1947, during which two screenwriters find and read a rejected screenplay-of-the-mind. This script is set in the year 2108, a century after nuclear war has destroyed America and bathed the few survivors in hard radiation, and makes up the bulk of the novel. But nothing is made of its wooden complexities.

The other problem with the book is hope. A ship from unscathed New Zealand visits California. A shy biologist, Dr Poole, is captured by the Californians, who worship Belial (as the Arch-Vicar explains in one of Huxley's best discussion scenes) because He has won. He has managed to persuade western humanity to believe in Progress: "Progress— the theory that you can get something for nothing; the theory that you can gain in one field without paying for your gain in another . . . the theory that you know what's going to happen fifty years from now."

The vicar goes on to demonstrate his case about the parasitic relationship of humanity to the planet with a scathing diatribe on overpopulation and the ecological devastation that follows (as indeed it has). He describes Belial's triumph in terms that seem prescient in 1993: the normalisation of atrocity; the lust to punish those who have already been punished; the addiction to nationalism. It all seems definitive enough for one book.

But love comes to Professor Poole, and a sense that Gaia herself endures beneath the apeish filth. He and his woman escape in the end, pausing for a moment of mythical circularity at the tomb of the man who wrote the screenplay they are characters in.

By 1948, in other words, Huxley was beginning to flinch from the zero horizon that lies at the end of the truest science-fiction texts of the century. It is a view, one supposes, that is difficult to bear. And a decade later, he was talking about the predictive accuracy of *Brave New World* as though details mattered.

In prophecy, they do not matter a whit. In the prophetic literature of the 20th century, it is not predictions—accuracies or bloopers about the next technological fix—that hold the attention or focus the vision.

Nowadays, it is the intimation that we will not get out of this time alive that shapes our sense of vision. It is a knowing terror that the great wheel will stall.

CHAPTER 3

The Art and Technique of Aldous Huxley

READINGS ON
BRAVE NEW WORLD

Creating the Plot

Guinevera A. Nance

Huxley considered *Brave New World* a difficult book to write, reports Guinevera A. Nance. A complex satire of a projected future, it offers no easy answers for the problems it raises. Nance describes how Huxley built his plot through irony, farce, exposition, and shifting points of view. Besides her book *Aldous Huxley*, from which this essay is excerpted, Nance is also coauthor of a study of Philip Roth.

Brave New World has been regarded as the archetypal dystopia[1] and as the "most influential anti-utopian novel of the twentieth century."[2] At the time he was writing the book, Huxley thought of it as a difficult piece of work—a novel on the "horror of the Wellsian Utopia and a revolt against it." Earlier, in *Point Counter Point*, he had satirized H.G. Wells's view of an inevitably progressive future; in *Brave New World* he sets out to show what a future that is the culmination of certain aspects of the twentieth century would be like. Projecting, for example, the results of this century's fascination with science and with mechanization into "Utopian infinity," he imagines a future in which human beings are scientifically engineered and mass-produced as easily and with as much standardization as one of Henry Ford's automobiles. Purely from the standpoint of efficiency and stability, this world of A.F. (After Ford) 632 represents an advance over the one Huxley is trying to warn; but in terms of freedom and full humanity, it is a version of the hell that Huxley, through Rampion in *Point Counter Point*, predicts as the outcome of industrialism and Americanization. Such a hell materializes, as Rampion foresees, "in the name of science, progress, and human happiness.". . .

1. Chad Walsh, *From Utopia to Nightmare* (New York: Harper & Row, 1962), 112. 2. George Kateb, *Utopia and Its Enemies* (New York: Free Press of Glencoe, 1963), 126.

Huxley moves slowly into plot in this novel, devoting the first two chapters to an explanation of the principle mechanisms of social control: eugenics/dysgenics, neo-Pavlovian conditioning, and hypnopaedia. A great deal of exposition is required to locate the reader in this strange world of the future, and Huxley handles it deftly through the device of a guided tour in which the various functions of the London Hatchery and Conditioning Centre are detailed for a troop of students. Along with the students, the reader follows the guide through the several factory-like rooms in which conveyors unceasingly move forward with their "load of future men and women."

In the third chapter, Huxley introduces Mustapha Mond, Resident Controller for Western Europe, and shifts to a montage technique of rapidly alternating scenes. Mond, the only character in the novel with a thorough knowledge of history (despite his assertion of the Fordian dictum that "history is bunk"), carries the exposition in this chapter. His function here is twofold: first, to recount the historical context of the World State; second, to contrast the present with the past, which he attempts to do in such a way as to make conditions before the advent of the World State seem undesirable. Alternating with his exposition are scenes in which the Hatchery's off-duty workers prepare for the diversions they have been conditioned to enjoy. Their talk of going to the Feelies or to play Obstacle Golf or of "having" a new sexual partner is juxtaposed for ironic effect with Mond's recitation of the horrors of the past. While he tells of the "appalling dangers of family life" in the age when there were mothers and fathers and sexual exclusiveness, the workers discuss the need to become more promiscuous in order to be seen as conventional; for in this new era, "every one belongs to every one else" according to the hypnopaedic proverb, and nonexclusiveness is the norm.

THE PLOT COMES INTO FOCUS

It is through the conversations taking place in the workers' dressing rooms that two of the leading characters and the plot begin to come into focus. Lenina Crowne, an especially "pneumatic" Beta who is clearly the product of the culture and her class, is discussing with her friend Fanny (also named Crowne) her plan to interrupt a four month's stint with only one lover by accepting Bernard Marx's invitation to visit a Savage Reservation. Simultaneously, in another changing room, Bernard Marx listens resentfully to a discussion of Lenina Crowne's sexual attributes as one man recommends her to another. Marx's reaction is partially jealousy and partially resistance to the rules of promiscuity. More diminutive than his Alpha Plus status would dictate, he envies the men of his caste their assurance and unself-conscious superiority—their success at having as many women as they want. At the same time, he is alienated enough from the social system to be slightly revolted by the normal practice of nonexclusive, impersonal sex. He sees Lenina's carefree sexuality as a degradation and wishes for something now considered taboo: a relationship founded on emotional intimacy.

In a society that insists on divorcing sex and emotion, Lenina is well adjusted. It is Bernard who is maladjusted. He is another of Huxley's eccentrics, but, ironically, his peculiarities are those of a sane man. The problem is that he lives in an insane world. His penchant for solitude and his preference for reality over *soma*-induced unreality make him suspect in this topsy-turvy society that prizes the community more than the individual and happiness more than truth. But the real sign of his unorthodoxy is his interest in cultivating his emotions. Like many of Huxley's characters, Bernard is emotionally infantile; however, in his case it is the result of cultural conditioning and a requirement of social conformity. So when he tells Lenina that he wants "to know what passion is" and "to feel something strongly," he is consciously rebelling against the system that allows some of its subjects to be adults intellectually but requires them to be "infants where feeling and desire are concerned."

Yet for all his brave talk and little acts of defiance, Bernard is not a hero and poses no real challenge to the system. . . . Bernard is not up to the task of living as "an adult all the time," as he puts it. However, he and his friend Helmholtz Watson, whose superior mental ability also sets him apart, serve a critical function in the first half or so of the novel in being the only dissenters against the order of things.

THE CONTRARY PERSPECTIVE

In addition, Bernard functions as the avenue through which Huxley introduces into the narrative the single perspective that is completely contrary to those prevalent in the World State—the point of view of the Savage, whose unique culture has been concocted from Indian primitivism and Shake-spearean sophistication. Once the Savage takes over the role of providing the antithetical perspective, Huxley can largely dispense with Bernard as a dissenting voice. In the last portion of the book, Marx becomes an increasingly unsympathetic character and the object of scathing satire. For example, when his role as guardian of the Savage gives him unprecedented prominence, his dissatisfaction with society dissipates. As the authorial voice of the novel satirically states: "Success went fizzily to Bernard's head, and in the process completely reconciled him . . . to a world which, up till then, he had found very unsatisfactory."

Even if Bernard were more inclined to keep up his resistance, he and Helmholtz can only go so far because their conditioning has created boundaries they cannot cross. As Mustapha Mond explains, "each one of us . . . goes through life inside a bottle." An Alpha's bottle may be, relatively speaking, enormous, and within it he may have a sense of autonomy; but he still has limits confining him. Only someone from outside the culture and its conditioning can present, if not a challenge, at least a complete contrast. The Savage from the New Mexico reservation represents that contrast. As Peter Firchow observes in his *The End of Utopia*, the appearance of the Savage in the new world "brings about the confrontation of the individual natural man with the artificial society of unnatural men."[3]

JOHN SAVAGE IS NOT A "NOBLE SAVAGE"

Huxley's use of a savage as his principal critic of the civilization crafted through science has the effect of recalling Rousseau's Noble Savage and the whole context of the romantic idealization of the natural man. The reminder turns out to be mostly ironic, however, since Huxley is unprepared to follow the romantic primitivists in asserting the innate goodness of man; nor is he convinced that urbanity is particularly bad. He does share the romantic's suspicion of progress, and it is such a suspicion that prompted the writing of *Brave New World*. But the central irony in Huxley's evocation of the Noble Savage idea is that although John Savage, as he comes to be called, fits the romantic prototype

---

3. Peter Edgerly Firchow, *The End of Utopia: A Study of Aldous Huxley's Brave New World* (Lewisburg: Bucknell University Press, 1984), 89.

in that he has a natural dignity and intelligence, he is not a savage.

Born in the wilds of New Mexico, the progeny of parents with origins in the new world, the Savage lives as a stranger among the Pueblo Indians. Although he tries to join the Indians in their tribal rituals, his white skin and blue eyes accentuate his difference, and he is excluded from the life of the reservation. This isolation from the primitive culture, plus his thorough grounding in the works of Shakespeare, account for his being in many ways more civilized than the inhabitants of the new world.

Naturally, the Savage is also set apart in his nobility from the Indians, whom Huxley does nothing to romanticize. If anything, he exaggerates the squalor in which they live and the brutality of their superstitions. As Huxley depicts it, the reservation embodies the horrors of past ages that Mond describes earlier in the novel—the filth, decrepitude, disease, death, sexual possessiveness, and familial perversions. Its one advantage is that it allows for the freedom to suffer and to be unhappy.

An outcast in primitive society, the Savage enthusiastically accepts Bernard's invitation to return with him to the "Other Place," which he has idealized from scraps of stories his mother has told him of the civilized world. He greets the prospect of going to London with Miranda's speech in the fifth act of *The Tempest*:

> O, wonder!
> How many goodly creatures are there here!
> How beauteous mankind is! O brave new world
> That has such people in't! (V.i. 181–84)

Like Miranda, the Savage is an innocent and unaware of the irony in this remark. Unlike Miranda, he eventually discovers the irony as he sees the discrepancy between the description and the reality to which it refers. But in this initial utterance of hope and joy, the Savage is as oblivious to Bernard's undercutting question "Hadn't you better wait till you actually see the new world?" as Miranda is to Prospero's more matter-of-fact statement, "'Tis new to thee" (V. i. 185).

Subsequent repetitions of the "O brave new world" refrain serve as something of a gauge of the Savage's reaction to civilized life. Joyful expectation turns to disgust as he encounters the "wonders" of an educational system that teaches the Malthusian Drill (for the correct application of contraceptives) and Death Conditioning and forbids Shakespeare; of the "Feelies," a sensory cinematic experience in which the audience can not only see a rather pornographic modern-day rendition of *Othello* called *Three Weeks in a Helicopter* but feel the stereoscopic kisses; or of the identical Bokanovsky Group workers that, conditioned to be dwarfed and deformed, staff the factories. Yet despite his growing sense of the irony of the Shakespearean litany, which he repeats almost unconsciously, he resolves to hold fast to his childhood vision of the paradisiacal Other Place. His attempt to separate the ideal and the real works until the death of his mother, when he is forced to face the devaluation of the individual in the new society. This realization is brought about first by the blasé reaction of the schoolchildren to Linda's death and, second, by John's confrontation with science's tribute to uniformness, the Bokanovsky Group—or, in this case, two groups of eighty-four identical Deltas each. The horror of such sameness and stupidity breaks into the Savage's consciousness, and the inappropriateness of his involuntary "How many goodly creatures are there here" makes a mockery of his idealism.

CHALLENGE AND AFFIRMATION

To this point, Miranda's speech has served to express joy and wonderment, to trigger childhood memories of paradise, to mock the Savage's idealism. Its final function is as a challenge and an affirmation of the possibility of transforming the world the Savage sees as hell into the utopian heaven of his dreams. That shift from derision to challenge takes place as he watches the distribution of *soma* to the Deltas and thinks:

> "O brave new world, O brave new world . . ." In his mind the singing words seemed to change their tone. They had mocked him through his misery and remorse, mocked him with how hideous a note of cynical derision! Fiendishly laughing, they had insisted on the low squalor, the nauseous ugliness of the nightmare. Now, suddenly, they trumpeted a call to arms. "O brave new world!" Miranda was proclaiming the possibility of loveliness, the possibility of transforming even the nightmare into something fine and noble. "O brave new world!" It was a challenge, a command.

The Savage responds to the challenge by hurling the Deltas' daily ration of *soma* out the window and berating them for their infantilism. For although he proclaims freedom as his mission, compassion quickly turns to hatred for the witless creatures he has come to save. He is joined in the ensuing melee by Bernard, who hesitates on the fringes of the battle in an "agony of indecision," and Helmholtz Watson, who plunges enthusiastically into the fracas with the Deltas and the police in gas masks and actually seems to be set free by this act of self-determination.

The farcical nature of this scene, with Helmholtz and the Savage punching away at the howling Deltas and Bernard running about under the pretense of helping, contrasts sharply with the succeeding major episode, in which the three renegades are confronted by the Controller, Mustapha Mond. Their different reactions reflect their fundamental differences in character. Learning that he may be exiled to an island populated by others who have exhibited antisocial tendencies, Bernard pleads obsequiously on his own behalf, blaming everything on Helmholtz and the Savage. While Bernard seems to have shrunk in stature, Helmholtz appears to have grown. He speaks to the Controller with assurance and earns his respect when he requests that the island to which he is exiled have a "thoroughly bad climate." As a writer intent on exploring the possibilities of his creativity, he chooses a bracing climate in the belief that it will stimulate his imagination. The novel leaves the impression that his banishment to the Falkland Islands will turn out to be the making of this would-be poet.

THE CENTRAL POINT: FREEDOM VS. HAPPINESS

Even more than Helmholtz, the Savage meets the Controller confidently, and his ability to engage in a debate with Mond as an intellectual equal sets him apart from his supposedly more civilized companions. The dialogue between the two of them is the raison d'être of this episode, which takes up two chapters. Through their conversation, Huxley focuses on the central problem that *Brave New World* is set up to explore: the extent to which happiness must necessarily exclude freedom and to which freedom must include unhappiness. The new-world civilization is predicated on the conviction that happiness and freedom are mutually exclusive and that happiness is the greater good. To prove the benefits of such an assumption, Mond points to the positive aspects of his society—it is stable and peaceful; its citizens are safe and happy, free of the deleterious effects of passion, unfulfilled desires, old age, and disease. When questioned more directly by the Savage about the place of art, science, and religion in the society, Mond explains that these have been sacrificed in the interest of comfort and happiness. Instead of high art, there are the Feelies, the scent organ, and synthetic music; instead of scientific inquiry, there is scientific orthodoxy; instead of religion, there are the Solidarity Services. Beauty, truth, and God are incompatible with machinery and universal happiness, but, Mond contends, so are evils such as decrepitude, disease, and the fear of death.

The Savage does not reject the notion that an uncontrolled society will incorporate these evils; he simply chooses freedom, even with its attendant pain, over happiness without freedom. To the Controller's observation that in the new world they "prefer to do things comfortably," the Savage responds: "But I don't want comfort. I want God, I want poetry, I want real danger, I want freedom, I want goodness, I want sin." Mond points out to him that, in fact, he is "claiming the right to be unhappy," as well as the right "to grow old and ugly and impotent; the right to have syphilis and cancer; the right to have too little to eat; the right to be lousy; the right to live in constant apprehension of what may happen tomorrow; the right to catch typhoid; the right to be tortured by unspeakable pains of every kind." The Savage holds firm: "I claim them all."

This simple and noble line would have been a fitting conclusion to *Brave New World* had Huxley wished to assert the superiority of primitivism over scientific determinism, but that is not the case. Mond has the last word in the debate, responding to the Savage's declaration with a shrug and a detached "You're welcome." Further, in the final chapter, Huxley makes the Savage's brand of primitive religion, which involves abasement and self-flagellation for purification from sin, seem particularly ferocious and unappealing. Thus, he effectively undercuts any temptation the reader might have to give primitivism the edge. And as if to remove any doubt that what he has presented is, basically, a choice between two evils, the last scene in the novel is of the Savage, dead by his own hand, swinging like a compass from the ceiling of an abandoned lighthouse.

SECOND THOUGHTS: A THIRD ALTERNATIVE

Fifteen or so years later, Huxley felt that the Savage's being offered "only two alternatives, an insane life in Utopia, or the life of a primitive in an Indian village, a life more human in some respects, but in others hardly less queer and abnormal" was a defect in the novel. In his foreword to the 1946 Collected Edition of *Brave New World*, he indicates that at the time the book was written he found both amusing and possibly true the idea that "human beings are given free will in order to choose between insanity on the one hand and lunacy on the other." But between the early thirties and the mid-forties, Huxley came to believe in the possibility of sanity; and in the foreword, he projects the kind of community that might result from devotion to this ideal. He says that the community's economics "would be decentralist and Henry-Georgian, politics Kropotkinesque and co-operative. Science and technology would be used as though, like the Sabbath, they had been made for man, not (as at present and still more so in the *Brave New World*) as though man were to be adapted and enslaved to them. Religion would be the conscious and intelligent pursuit of man's Final End, the unitive knowledge of the immanent Tao or Logos, the transcendent Godhead or Brahman." This outline of a utopian society takes on form and substance a decade and a half later in *Island.*

Using Fantasy to Criticize Reality

C.S. Ferns

By using fantasy, science fiction, and satire to create an exaggerated world, writes C.S. Ferns, Huxley encourages the reader to make his or her own connections between the fantasy of *Brave New World* and conditions in the real world. This subtle approach is more effective than direct criticism of such problems as overconsumption and the promiscuity and irresponsibility of the younger generation. C.S. Ferns is the author of *Aldous Huxley: Novelist*, from which this essay is taken.

It is to satire that Huxley turns in *Brave New World*. . . . Instead of trying to integrate a criticism of society and its values with a realistic depiction of them, he elects to attack them from the outset, and there can be little doubt that his critique gains considerably in force and cogency as a result. . . . In *Brave New World* the limitations of amorality and hedonism are exposed by the grotesque lengths they are carried to, so that there is scarcely any need for explicit comment. . . .

ALLOWING READERS TO FIND THE PARALLELS BETWEEN FANTASY AND REALITY

Once Huxley abandons his attempts to offer a realistic portrayal of society, his vision of the world becomes considerably more persuasive. Accepting the world of the distant future . . . as being the author's invention, the reader tacitly admits the author's right to lay down the rules for the worlds he creates. Instead of aspiring to portray a world which his readers also know, and are liable to see quite differently, Huxley presents his vision as a fantasy. While parallels with the real world are hinted at, it is left to the reader to draw them: instead of insisting that life is like *this*, and thus incurring the resistance of readers who feel pressurized into accepting an account of reality which they do not believe to be accurate, Huxley, through his use of the medium of fantasy, is able to imply his own views of what constitutes reality with a far greater chance of their being accepted—after all, if the reader detects parallels between the fantasy and reality, it merely shows that the connections are already present in the reader's mind.

Additionally, Huxley exploits the fact that the worlds he creates are *different*, foreign to the reader's experience, to arouse curiosity as to their nature. The more bizarre the events or setting, the more eager the reader becomes to find some kind of ordering explanation, with the result that the explanations that *are* offered are all the more likely to be accepted. And while he overtly answers the reader's questions, Huxley is able covertly to comment on the real world, with the advantage that whereas in a realistic context his explanations, his commentary might be rejected out of hand, in the context of a fantasy the instinct of rejection is usually outweighed by the feeling of curiosity satisfied. . . .

In a fantastic context Huxley is able to resolve many of the difficulties created by his confused understanding of the relations between the individual and society. Indeed, the principal theme of *Brave New World* is precisely the conflict between the individual and society—a society which, because it is his own invention, he is able to understand and hence portray far more clearly. Although his view of society remains a pessimistic one, the tale of Bernard, Helmholz, and the Savage's confrontation with and defeat by authority provides [a] kind of backbone for Huxley's satiric vision of the world of the future. . . .

PLAYING AN ELABORATE GAME WITH READERS

Huxley not only recovers, but develops the cool, ironic, detached tone which was one of the most attractive features of his early fiction. In *Brave New World*, for example, there is evident from the very outset the characteristic liveliness which, in *Point Counter Point*, seemed to have been sacrificed in the interests of a more realistic approach. With the opening words of *Brave New World*—'A squat grey building of only thirty-four storeys. . .'—Huxley begins playing an elaborate game with his readers, alternating the assumption that they are, of course, familiar with the kind of world implied by '*only* thirty-four storeys', with the provision of information clearly designed to satisfy his audience's appetite for details concerning a world with which they are unfamiliar: information, for example, about the absurd technological features of the world he has created, such as the feelies, scent organs, escalator squash, electromagnetic golf, and so forth. Indeed, there could scarcely be a stronger contrast than that between the wit and panache of the opening sequence of *Brave New World*, with its vivid presentation of an imaginary society, culminating in a sense of nightmarish confusion induced by the accelerating cross-cutting between the various narrative lines, and the resolutely drab naturalism of the first scene in *Point Counter Point*, which led Wyndham Lewis to complain, with some justification, that Huxley had adopted 'the very accent of the newspaper serial'. Nor does the contrast end there: throughout *Brave New World* maintains a level of inventiveness, excitement, and energy which his realistic fiction never approaches.

Of course, part of the attraction of fantasy is that it allows the author to entertain his audience with novelties and inventions which are beyond the scope of a realistic approach, but Huxley uses the extra freedom which fantasy gives him for more than mere entertainment purposes. In both *Brave New World* and *After Many A Summer*, but particularly in the former, Huxley consistently exploits the reader's curiosity by integrating into the passages where he satisfies that curiosity a commentary on the real world, the world in which both he and the reader live. Take for example the early scene, where a group of Delta (low intelligence) infants are being conditioned into a hatred of books and flowers by the use of aversion therapy. The babies are first encouraged to crawl towards an attractive looking display of brightly coloured books and flowers, but on reaching it are then terrified by a combination of loud noises and electric shocks. At first sight it is a scene of wanton cruelty, conditioning for conditioning's sake—the infliction of pain and terror on young children is likely to arouse feelings of the most violent antipathy, and Huxley gives a lurid description of just that. As a result, the reader becomes anxious to learn the reason for this apparently motiveless cruelty, to hear the answer to the student's question—'"Why go to the trouble of making it psychologically impossible for Deltas to like flowers?"' (Books, obviously enough, might have a subversive and deconditioning effect.) It is this skilfully aroused curiosity which Huxley manipulates in order to give maximum effect to the critique of the consumer society which then follows. As the D.H.C., the official who has staged the demonstration of infant conditioning, explains:

> If the children were made to scream at the sight of a rose, that was on grounds of high economic policy. Not so very long ago. . . Gammas, Deltas, even Epsilons, had been conditioned to like flowers—flowers in particular and wild nature in general. The idea was to make them want to be going out into the country at every available opportunity, and so compel them to consume transport.

> 'And didn't they consume transport?' asked the student.

> 'Quite a lot,' the D.H.C. replied. 'But nothing else.'

Because 'a love of nature keeps no factories busy' a policy decision was taken to 'abolish the love of nature, at any rate among the lower classes. . .' They are still encouraged to travel to the country, of course—transport must still be consumed—but only in order to play sports requiring the use of elaborate manufactured apparatus. Human beings are conditioned by the society which manufactures consumer goods into a preference for the artificial, the complicated, and the expensive over the simple, the natural, and the cheap.

The parallel with our own society is too obvious to be missed, but the fantastic context enables Huxley to present his views far more effectively than he could have done in a more realistic setting; by making the explanation which the reader's curiosity demands as grotesque, vivid, and horrifying as possible, Huxley manages to avoid the invidious earnestness which is always liable to attend overt explanations of a realistically presented world. Just as Jonathan Swift used the mechanisms of the traveller's tale in *Gulliver's Travels* to secure the attention of his audience, so that he might communicate his own views about society, so Huxley, in *Brave New World* relies on the attractions of Science Fiction to obtain a hearing for the message he wishes to convey.

ECONOMY OF EXPRESSION PROVIDES A POWERFUL FOCUS

Within the fantastic context, Huxley is also able to achieve a far greater economy and forcefulness of expression. In both *Point Counter Point* and *Eyeless in Gaza* human folly and weakness are illustrated by the accumulation of a large number of individual examples of undesirable attitudes and behaviour. But the drawback of such an approach is that the preponderance of negatively presented characters creates an imbalance which is at odds with Huxley's pretensions to be offering an objective and realistic account of the world.

In *Brave New World*, however, Huxley avoids the multiplication of individual examples, instead achieving a far more striking effect by linking together the most incompatible attitudes and behaviour, and using the resultant incongruity to expose their mutual absurdity. In *Point Counter Point*, where it is clear that Huxley rejects not only the values and conventional morality of the older generation, but also the irresponsibility and amorality of the younger, this dual rejection creates a certain confusion: there are perhaps too many targets for Huxley to hope to be able to hit them all. . . .

In *Brave New World*, by contrast, simply by *identifying* the promiscuity and irresponsibility of the younger generation with conventional morality, Huxley succeeds in bringing into focus both the objects of his attack.

In *Brave New World* any form of sexual behaviour *other* than promiscuity is socially unacceptable, and by making promiscuity respectable, Huxley deprives it of its aura of daring and excitement, thereby exposing its emptiness as a way of life. At the same time convention, once it is seen to uphold values to which it is normally opposed, no longer appears to be some kind of absolute standard, but merely a reflection of the unthinking assumptions of the day. The appalling inanity of the conversation in the helicopter between Henry and Lenina, where both complacently parrot the sentiments they have been conditioned into accepting, or the triteness of the synthetic folk wisdom enshrined in the proverbs everyone uses ('a gramme is better than a damn', 'one cubic centimetre cures ten gloomy sentiments'), stand out because of the unfamiliarity of the underlying assumptions, but the real target is clearly the fatuity of the popular beliefs of Huxley's own day. Few readers are likely to be free of their own unthinking assumptions—assumptions which are not thought about because of their very familiarity: it is the *unfamiliarity* of the endlessly reiterated sentiments in *Brave New World* that highlights the extent to which people's beliefs are unthinking and conditioned. It would be hard for any reader to ignore the relevance to the present world of high technology, mass communications, and advertising of the depiction of a society where everyone's opinions are acquired during their sleep.

EXPLOITING INCONGRUITY FOR SATIRIC EFFECT

Huxley similarly exploits incongruities for satiric effect by linking technology and religion. By making the deity ('Our Ford') a motor manufacturer, Huxley satirizes the way in which technological and scientific progress is worshipped as an end in itself: in the society of the future the salient qualities of the machine—efficiency and productivity—have become the cardinal virtues of mankind. At the same time, religion is exposed as mere escapist ritual; the pomp and dignity normally associated with religious ceremonies are deflated by the ludicrous rites of Ford-worship, solemnized by such officials as the Arch Community-Songster of Canterbury.

Incongruity, too, is at the root of Huxley's portrayal of the relations between Lenina and the Savage, in which both the irresponsible hedonism of the former and the romantic illusions of the latter are ridiculed. The Savage's intense emotions, dressed up in grand Shakespearian language, are rendered farcical by the object of his love. For an object is precisely what Lenina is, the product of conditioning rather than a person in her own right. Yet by her very vacuousness she helps to expose what a great deal of romantic love is all about—the projection onto someone else of a private fantasy, rather than a genuine attempt to *know* them. Lenina shows up this element of projection so clearly because she is, so to speak, a blank screen. On the other hand, ridiculous though the Savage is made to look, the fact that he has real emotions at all, however mis-directed, highlights the blandness and shallowness of the relations which the citizens of Brave New World accept as normal.

Fantasy, then, is a medium which enables Huxley to convey what he sees as unpalatable truths about the society in which he lives, and to do so with the maximum vividness and clarity. Yet at the same time, because the fantasy world he creates is so nightmarish, horrible in a far more definite and concrete way than is the case with the worlds described in his realistic fiction, some form of genuine opposition to it becomes possible. In *Brave New World* we find individuals in conflict with their environment, and Huxley makes good use of the sympathy and sense of identification which the reader feels with their struggles.

EXPLOITING THE READER'S SYMPATHIES

This is particularly noticeable in the case of Bernard, who is the first character encountered by the reader to possess good healthy neuroses, resentments and feelings of inferiority in the midst of a world of mindless, well-adjusted happiness— the first character, in other words, with whom it is possible to identify. However, just as Swift does in *Gulliver's Travels*, Huxley exploits the reader's sympathies for satiric effect. Much as the reader experiences a jolt when, having loftily identified with Gulliver's contempt for the pretensions of the little men of Lilliput, he finds himself condemned in similar terms by the gigantic King of Brobdingnag, so Huxley, having first established Bernard as a sympathetic character by making him a cogent critic of the dreadful world he lives in, then makes the reader uncomfortably aware of the self-betrayal involved when he succumbs to the lures of worldly success. Like Illidge in *Point Counter Point*, Bernard is hostile to society primarily because he is unable to succeed in its terms. But whereas Illidge is essentially unsympathetic, seen from outside, and also an unsuccessful creation, due to Huxley's attempt to embody in him some sort of portrait of a *typical* revolutionary, Bernard works as a character simply by virtue of the sympathy he engenders. Rather than attempting to discredit a particular ideological attitude by a jaundiced portrayal of one of its adherents, Huxley sets out, in his characterization of Bernard, to make his readers ask themselves whether or not they, too, might not be deterred from opposing what they knew to be wrong by the same bribe of success which Bernard accepts. Illidge, in the end, is merely a pathetic figure, whereas Bernard, whose criticisms of society we are likely to share, forces us to ask whether we do not also share his weaknesses.

Similarly, with Helmholz and the Savage, the sympathy engendered by their opposition to a distasteful society highlights rather than disguises the inadequate nature of their resistance to it. What is emphasized is not so much the fact that they are defeated, with the Savage committing suicide and Helmholz being exiled, but the nature of their defeat. The Savage's hatred of society is rooted in a self-indulgent romanticism and an asceticism which is obsessional and masochistic; Helmholz's dissatisfaction stems from frustrated creative aspirations: neither is able to live the kind of life he wants. But in the end their opposition dissolves, with both of them taking what is in fact the easiest way out—the Savage commits suicide, and Helmholz acquiesces in his exile with something like pleasurable anticipation. Yet in sympathizing with their opposition, we are once again forced to ask whether their weaknesses, their failures would not also be ours. In effect, Huxley presents a world which is the logical conclusion of what he sees as the direction in which our society is going—a direction in which he believes it ought not to go. And while we, of course, would agree that the world he presents is undesirable, it is perhaps Huxley's most significant achievement that in *Brave New World* he makes us examine more closely the nature of our opposition to and disagreement with the assumptions of that world.

chemical and technical details. Huxley's manner of repeating the Director's words suggests that he, the author, and we, the readers, share familiarity with these details to which the young trainees are being introduced, as well as a sophisticated rapport which excludes both Director and trainees. This is an excellent way of passing off the most startling of innovations as if it were commonplace (thus anchoring us in the world of AF 632), while at the same time keeping the characters in the sphere of satire. The method also preserves Huxley from having to dwell at tedious length upon the techniques of incubation and having to invent the uninventable. For instance, 'the technique for preserving the excised ovary alive and actively developing' can be referred to in passing, with the implication that we either are thoroughly acquainted with these matters or would not now want to bother our heads with them.

COOL MOCKERY

Huxley's attitude in the passage which I have quoted is, broadly speaking, the attitude of much of the book. Most aspects of the novel are treated cooly and sometimes with seeming offhandedness, however alien or shocking they might be. A tone of mockery governs the presentation both of innovations and of characters' behaviour. . . . Since the new techniques have not improved human nature, both the techniques and human nature can be mocked. In so far as *Brave New World* is a parody of *Men Like Gods*, the parody consists not only in a portrait of a spiritual decline from the standards of the twentieth century but also, and perhaps mainly, in the fact that people, in spite of momentous changes in environment, often behave in thoroughly familiar ways.[1] Whereas in Wells's imagination the distant future or a contemporary world in a different dimension from ours, always belongs to radically different beings (god-like Utopians, bestial Morlocks, ennervated Eloi), Huxley's characters manifest all the usual vanities and selfishnesses. Such a remarkable change as the disappearance of family life is principally shown as having altered the objects of taboo or scatology. The scientifically-determined caste system has not

1. See *Writers at Work*, The *Paris Review* Interviews, Second Series, (int. Van Wyck Brooks), Secker & Warburg, 1963, p. 165: 'Well that started out as a parody of H.G. Wells' *Men Like Gods*, but gradually it got out of hand and turned into something quite different from what I'd originally intended. As I became more and more interested in the subject, I wandered farther and farther away from my original purpose.'

abolished snobbery in the upper classes: for instance, a pretty girl is prouder to be the sexual partner of an Alpha-Plus than of a mere Alpha.

The opening chapter illustrates this point quite clearly, because in it the exposition of Bokanovsky's Process and accompanying techniques proceeds via a piece of social comedy of the usual Huxleyan sort. The Director is a pompous administrator; Henry Foster is the regular naïvely clever scientist, and the students unquestioningly take notes in a time-honoured manner. Sycophancy, gullibility, and various comic trappings of any hierarchical institution at any period are all still in evidence.

But these attributes are conveyed with brevity. . . . For once, and very suitably, Huxley does not contemplate at length the qualities he is describing. The tone of dispatch is present even in the opening sentences.

> A squat grey building of only thirty-four stories. Over the main entrance the words, CENTRAL LONDON HATCHERY AND CONDITIONING CENTRE, and, in a shield, the World State's motto, COMMUNITY, IDENTITY, STABILITY.

The promptitude here, the businesslike absence of verbs, is calculated to reduce the sense of something wonderful being described. It is part of Huxley's purpose throughout the book to offer the marvellous as though it were commonplace, and so one almost misses the information (which in most of his other novels he would typically have stressed) that the building has 'only' thirty-four stories, and almost accepts without question the function of the building, the fact that there is a World State, the nature of the motto, and, perhaps, its not being in Latin.

Similarly, for all the proper length of the second paragraph Huxley makes no fuss over the symbolic mortuary quality with which he invests, of all places, the Fertilizing Room.

> The enormous room on the ground floor faced towards the north. Cold for all the summer beyond the panes, for all the tropical heat of the room itself, a harsh thin light glared through the windows, hungrily seeking some draped lay figure, some pallid shape of academic goose-flesh, but finding only the glass and nickel and bleakly shining porcelain of a laboratory. Wintriness responded to wintriness. The overalls of the workers were white, their hands gloved with a pale corpse-coloured rubber. The light was frozen, dead, a ghost. Only from the yellow barrels of the microscopes did it borrow

a certain rich and living substance, lying along the polished tubes like butter, streak after luscious streak in long recession down the work tables.

. . . The tone of the first chapter likewise continues to prevail in the second; a tone which by ridiculing the people and the environment mitigates shock but produces its own—and, it may be, more lasting—kind of effectiveness.

However, the method of the first two chapters cannot be pursued for long. Though Huxley is conveying information in a concise way he clearly cannot by this means expound almost every important feature of his society before the main plot begins. Consequently, in Chapter Three he adopts a fresh and exhilarating technique which may as well be called 'cutting'. . . .

CUTTING FROM SCENE TO SCENE

Huxley often makes implicit points (for all his general explicitness) by arranging meaningful contiguities. It seems likely that this procedure was not simply a tactic, but a product of his very cast of mind. In the third chapter of *Brave New World* a method of this kind is used more blatantly than elsewhere, and is used not solely to offer ironic contrasts but also to tell the reader a great deal in a short time.

The manoeuvres are very smooth. At the opening of the chapter the minor story continues as the Director leads his party of students into the garden of the Central London Hatchery and Conditioning Centre. All is proceeding as we have come to expect when the students observe children at play and even when they come face to face with Mustapha Mond, the Resident Controller for Western Europe. Then abruptly the scene changes and for a few short paragraphs we are told about workers coming off duty. This is the first mention of Bernard Marx and Lenina Crowne whose story is now unobtrusively beginning. The camera, as it were, now moves back again to the garden where Mustapha Mond is starting to explain *ex cathedra* why the past was bad. History, though bunk, serves to remind the higher castes, who alone know anything about it, of the felicities of the present.

The chapter now proceeds by a succession of separated paragraphs which alternately consist of Mustapha Mond's remarks (or the author's gloss upon them) and conversations taking place in the men's and women's changing rooms. While Henry Foster and a colleague, overheard by a resentful Bernard Marx, are discussing the sexual desirability of Lenina Crowne, Lenina herself is disclosing her frame of mind to a friend, and outside in the garden the Controller is discoursing on the bygone evils of family and parenthood. As the chapter unfolds we learn through the Controller's words nearly all we need to know about present customs and attitudes and the history of the past seven hundred years. Meanwhile, present attitudes are being exemplified by the other two conversations, and attention is being paid to two leading characters. . . .

RECONCILING OPPOSITES

In Chapters Seven and Eight Huxley achieves effects which are diametrically the opposite of the effects produced in most of the rest of the book. Partly in this way he arranges a perfect aesthetic and philosophical balance between the utopian and the primitive horns of the dilemma; between the minimization of suffering and the positive search for suffering. Hence the inclusion of this scene of penitential torture, which of course foreshadows John's self-flagellation and suicide in the final chapter. These central scenes are not unnecessary pieces of self-indulgence on the author's part, for Huxley, as so often, is seeking to reconcile opposites. Consequently, there is contemplation, restrained not loosely relished, of the scene: the man clad as an animal; the loneliness of the boy; the sympathetic but unnerving noises from the onlookers; the sound of the whip; the sight of the blood. Although this is a portrait of what Huxley in the foreword of 1946 calls 'lunacy', a 'life . . . hardly less queer and abnormal' than the Brave-New-Worldian life, it is not a comic portrait. One form of lunacy is funny but the other form is not. In these central chapters of *Brave New World*, there is a reversal of mood and tone. The eye moving along the frieze takes in a series of rather alarmingly humorous scenes and then without warning is confronted with grotesqueness of a different and unfunny kind. From now on the reader's response to the book will be more ambiguous than it has been, and in this way his 'creative doubts', as I have called them, will grow to match those of the author.[2] . . .

2. This is what A.E. Dyson must have in mind when he writes: 'The novel is similar in structure to Book IV of Gulliver, particularly in that the direction the irony seems to be taking is devastatingly reversed half-way through, and everything thrown in the melting-pot again.' A.E. Dyson, 'Aldous Huxley and the Two Nothings', *Critical Quarterly*, Winter, 1961, p. 300.

The author has so designed this novel that from now on, that is for most of the second half, our response to the events is as uncertain as his own. The new society is meaningless, pointing to nothing outside or beyond itself, but happiness preponderates over misery; the alternatives are at best a search, in the way of Helmholtz Watson, or the apparently crazy pursuit of misery in the manner of the Savage.

Huxley's method is to propel us rather quickly, but not over-hastily, towards the long climactic scenes. Chapters Eleven and Twelve are thus divided into smallish sections in which, primarily, there is a renewal of social comedy as Bernard ignobly enjoys his brief period of popularity, Linda, the Savage's mother, sinks into a prolonged *soma*-holiday, and the Savage grows disgusted with civilized society. There is a good deal of Huxley's usual adept portraiture of the snobberies and vanities of social life, and there are also serio-comedic pictures of the conflict between two attitudes to concupiscence. John, loving Lenina more each day, welcomes his emotions but loathes his bodily appetites, while Lenina desiring John more and more, hates her emotions and seeks to lose them in sexual activity. Here again, or rather, as part of the same total problem, Huxley is dramatizing his own doubts, for he has always derided (with varying degrees of sympathy) both the torments of unsatisfied sexual yearnings and unimpeded sexual release. . . .

HUXLEY'S CONCERN WITH DEATH

Although the deaths in *Brave New World* are not treated with that overt or barely concealed horror and fascination that one finds in some of [his] other novels, they provide clear clues as to the precise nature of Huxley's concern. The farce at the Park Lane Hospital is a means of attending . . . [to] the problem of whether death really is the conquest of the soul by the body. Brave-New-Worldians assume—indeed, think they have proved—that an individual is the sum of the suggestions implanted into him, and, therefore, since he is bound to be reluctant to leave this happy life, it is humane to distract him in his last hours. The Savage, who welcomes suffering, is appalled by this procedure. No better means could be found of exactly opposing the happiness principle to the Final End principle. What Huxley is considering is the possibility that, if this life is all, then happiness may be the most reasonable aim and the Brave-New-Worldians may be right. Immortal longings can and perhaps should be scientifically removed. But if this life is not all (and even Mustapha Mond thinks that 'there quite probably is' a God), the society is undoubtedly as much in error as it appears to be. . . .

Artistically and as a means of best illustrating the theme the scenes at the hospital are in their proper place. As comedy they provide the hectic culmination of many preceding absurdities, and thematically they present the crux of the whole matter of the book. Now in place of comparatively sedate antics (I do not include the happenings at the reservation) we are presented with Linda dying as the music from the Super-Vox-Wurlitzeriana rises to a crescendo, as numerous identical children clamber in play over the neighbouring beds, and as the Savage weeps in horror and distress. The immediate aftermath of her death is the knockabout episode when the Savage throws boxes of *soma* pills out of the hospital window and fights with frenzied children and police in gas-masks. Huxley is here using the conventions of farce (for the scene resembles the high moments of a farce both in its situation and in its occurrences) to express ambiguities, because the actions of the Savage are as wrongheaded in their way as are the actions of the scientifically-conditioned participants. One senses from the tone of these episodes that here is no simple matter of one right-minded victim (or three victims, if we include Bernard Marx and Helmholtz Watson) versus many persecutors, but rather of two opposed forms of error, one of which, because it is perpetrated by a brave rebel, enlists our sympathies (but not very keenly). John is right in principle to cling to spiritual values, but he is clinging to the wrong values: the Brave-New-Worldians are right in principle to abolish the pains of death, but they have abolished them in the wrong ways.

Using Language in a World That Debases Language

David W. Sisk

Huxley has a great deal of fun with names and words, writes David W. Sisk, author of a book on the language used in *Brave New World* and other dystopias. Characters' names and the terms used by the World State's inhabitants offer layers of meaning. This is particularly ironic, notes Sisk, since Huxley is writing of a world where language has nearly completely lost all meaning.

Brave New World was Huxley's fifth novel, written at the peak of his literary powers. At the time of its publication, Huxley was the preeminent figure in the vanguard of English intellectual and literary culture. His name alone conveyed a mood of ironic social and literary criticism, reflecting his talent for propounding shocking new ideas while attacking works and theories he considered hopelessly outdated. . . .

A CONCERN WITH LANGUAGE

Huxley's concern with language substantially informs *Brave New World*. Baker argues that Huxley borrowed this concern from H.G. Wells's *When the Sleeper Wakes* (1899):[1]

> One feature of Wells's novel is especially characteristic of the dystopian narrative—the preoccupation with communications media and language. The [workers] are controlled by an elaborate system of propaganda, including a network of Babble Machines designed to implant "counter suggestions in the

---

1. In his Preface to volume 2 of *The Works of H.G. Wells*, Wells notes that the novel was first published in 1899 as *When the Sleeper Wakes*, and that in 1911, he "took the opportunity afforded by its reprinting to make a number of excisions and alterations" (1924, ix-x). For the Atlantic Edition, in which his Preface appears, he changed the title to *The Sleeper Awakes*.

cause of law and order" [Wells 1924, 392]. The oppressed
workers also speak a debased dialect. This motif of language
will recur in the dystopias of Zamiatin, Huxley, and Orwell,
only in more complexly subtle forms. (Baker 1990, 37)

Regardless of whether Huxley inherited his dystopic interest in the role of language from Wells, he certainly expressed it more subtly. *Brave New World* does not reveal a
government forcing a thought-restricting language on its
populace. Rather, Huxley shows us a society that engineers
its population from conception on and then fulfills all the desires that it has conditioned in them. The citizens of the
Brave New World State do not consider themselves repressed. They do not long for things that the State has done
away with. On the contrary, some words for outdated concepts still exist but have been debased into vapidity (*love*),
smutty humor (*marriage*) or even obscenity (especially the
term *mother*). As far as the vast majority of citizens are concerned, complete happiness and social harmony have been
brought about at no cost to themselves. Except in a handful
of malcontents like Helmholtz Watson and authority figures
like Mustapha Mond, there is no perception that social stability has been bought at a high price.

That price includes the destruction of history and the de-
terioration of language. . . .

"Worst of all, language has virtually lost its meaning and
few speakers in this model world of scientifically engineered
precision realize how unscientific and imprecise their words
really are" (Meckier 1969, 181). Doing away with literature
has severely affected the use of language. Other than insipid
popular music—"There ain't no Bottle in all the world like
that dear little Bottle of mine"—there are no models to guide
usage and no means available to expand vocabulary or experiment with structure. Human languages and other cultural differences have been severely reduced by the World
State, since stability requires mutual understanding between
different peoples. Some languages, like "Zuñi and Spanish
and Athapascan," are nearly extinct, surviving only in the
Savage Reservations, while others, including French, German, and Polish, are completely dead. Huxley has his tongue
firmly in cheek when he notes that "it was lucky that
Bernard didn't understand Zuñi." The Savage need not
speak Zuñi in order to keep secrets, his Shakespearean English being sufficiently impenetrable to those around him—

"for Ford's sake, John, talk sense. I can't understand a word you say" cries Lenina, to whom his references to *The Tempest* are nonsense.

PLAYING WITH NAMES

Brian Aldiss, who calls *Brave New World* "arguably the Western world's most famous science fiction novel," asks "Isn't one of the delights of [Huxley's dystopia], when all is said and pontificated, that it is told with a perfect balance of wit and humour?" (in Aldiss and Wingrove 1986, 184–85). Huxley repeatedly lightens the tone of his novel with the "agreeable weapons" of satiric witticisms, which amuse at first, until their full meaning becomes clear. One of the synchronous narratives in Chapter 3 finds Lenina Crowne talking to Fanny Crowne in the Hatchery's women's dressing rooms. The two are not related, "but as the [two billion] inhabitants of the planet had only ten thousand names between them, the coincidence was not particularly surprising." The reader may smile when thinking of the humorous situations that will inevitably occur given such a paucity of names, but a moment's thought makes one wonder why there are so few names for so many people. The answer, simply put, is that the World State removes another dangerous tendency toward individual identity by making sure that not even one's name distinguishes one from other citizens. Still, some names involve puns. For example, Henry *Foster* conducts ovarian research in the Hatchery, with the aim of producing increasing numbers of new workers. (Firchow suggests that Huxley may also be referring to Sir Michael Foster [1836–1907], a British embryologist who had been, like H.G. Wells, an assistant to Huxley's grandfather T.H. Huxley [46].) Similarly, Mustapha *Mond* is one of the ten World Controllers.[2] Huxley further satirizes a number of contemporary and historical individuals in the names he gives his characters:

> As in the old allegorical fables, Huxley gives many of his characters names which symbolize his particular *bêtes*

---

2. Kumar points out that "an especially important role is marked out for *Mustapha Mond.* His name not only plays on the fact that he is one of the ten World Controllers, but also takes a side-swipe at the nationalism symbolized by Attaturk [*sic*] and, more importantly, refers to Alfred Mond (the later Lord Melchett), the founder and dynamic chairman of the chemical firm I[mperial] C[hemical] I[ndustries]. Mond stands for the new giant conglomerates that were coming to dominate the industrial world. He is a particularly good choice on Huxley's part, not simply as one of the new breed of scientist-industrialist, but because both the left and the right were hailing the conglomerates enthusiastically as the latest and most progressive organizational form in the modern world: the right because they were a move towards 'rationalization,' the left because they were a halfway-house to nationalization (1987, 243)."

noires. Together, they add up to a fairly comprehensive indictment of western thought and achievement since the Enlightenment. . . . The Left gets a trouncing in Polly *Trotsky,* Sarojini *Engels,* Herbert *Bakunin,* Lenina Crowne, and Bernard *Marx.* For Huxley, Socialism and Marxism, as the latest variants of scientific rationalism, differed from other varieties only in their greater arrogance and fanaticism, a judgment the Russian Revolution and the new Soviet State had done nothing to shake. He naturally had no greater faith in right-wing dictators or large capitalists, who are rebuffed in *Benito* Hoover and *Primo* Mellon, the last also doubling for capitalists along with Morgana *Rothschild.* Technology gets its due in George *Edsel,* Joanna *Diesel,* and Clara *Deterding,* and science its brickbat in *Darwin* Bonaparte, *Bernard* Marx, and Helmholtz *Watson. Watson* is also Huxley's back-handed tribute to the founder of behaviourism in psychology, and therefore a key influence in the new society. (Kumar 1987, 243)

Huxley lampoons capitalists in *Morgana*'s name, suggesting J.P. Morgan, and one can hardly overlook Benito *Hoover* as an ironic jab at Herbert Hoover, president of the United States at the time of *Brave New World*'s composition and already infamous for asserting that "the business of America is business."[3] Darwin *Bonaparte* suggests another right-wing dictator of note, as does *Mustapha* Mond (recalling the Turkish nationalist leader Kemal Ataturk Mustapha). Social theorists and writers are criticized with names like Fifi *Bradlaugh* and *Jean-Jacques* Habibullah (whose last name may recall Habibullah Khan) (Firchow 1984, 83). Upon his arrival from Malpais, John is christened "The Savage," harking back to Rousseau—but John's nobility is matched by his fanatical inability to adapt to the society that he names the Brave New World, echoing Shakespeare.[4] Huxley damns Henry Ford and Ivan Pavlov by adopting their names directly, Ford as the World State's patron saint and Pavlov as the pioneer of the behavioral conditioning so necessary to the State. In fact, the Central London Hatchery contains an entire block of floors, the "Neo-Pavlovian Conditioning Rooms," given over to hypnopaedic and aversion conditioning. Huxley pokes at H.G. Wells by having Fanny Crowne refer to the "Dr. Wells" who advised her to undergo a Pregnancy Substitute.

3. Meckier calls Benito Hoover's name "an oxymoronic combination of capitalism and Fascism" (1969, 181). 4. Huxley puns here with the French *mal pays*—"evil country," "bad place." It certainly appears that way to Lenina. Yet despite their squalor, the Native Americans in Malpais still live their own lives, independent from the World State. Could Huxley thus be ironically undercutting the reader's preference for the true dystopia, the "bad place" of the Brave New World?

Huxley reserves his harshest treatment for another famous Fabian Socialist, George Bernard Shaw. To begin with, *Bernard* Marx is intellectually gifted but essentially a coward, unwilling to stand up for what he believes. Furthermore, the Director of Hatcheries explains that the first discovery of hypnopaedia occurred when a radio left on overnight broadcast Shaw declaiming on the subject of his own genius, an address that a young Polish boy wakes up repeating, despite not understanding English. The ironic dig is clear. Shaw's words are merely inconsequential babble, a judgment sealed by the fact that Shaw is "one of the very few whose works have been permitted to come down to us," as the Director notes. As Mond makes clear to the touring students, nearly all literature published before the year A.F. 150 has been suppressed; the fact that Shaw's works are not forbidden points to their essential harmlessness and their inability to disrupt conditioning.

Jerome Meckier suggests that at least one name that Huxley used is more gently ironic, more accusatory of society than of the individual to whom it belongs:

> Helmholtz Watson's name, a curious amalgam of Hermann Ludwig von Helmholtz (1821–1894), the German scientist, and Sir William Watson (1858–1935), an English poet, seems to imply that science and art are now united, but innocuously so, in the job of furnishing slogans for the state. In fact, the famous names of these characters form a pointed contrast to a World State that is simply one of Henry Ford's Detroit plants magnified many times. (1969, 181)

Meckier further argues that sporting with characters' names is meant to "remind the reader of similar linguistic witticisms in More's *Utopia* and Samuel Butler's *Erewhon*" (1983, 106). Huxley toys with some place names and names of landmarks as well, to ironic effect. Since all crosses have been cut in deference to Our Ford, London's Charing Cross has become Charing T, and as Bernard arrives at the Fordson Community Singery, he hears Big Henry, its clock-tower bell, toll the hour. Firchow concisely asserts Huxley's reason for making so much of names, which is

> not merely that from the perspective of distant time the concerns of the present fuse together into a single whole. . . . Rather, what Huxley seems to be implying is that all of the dynamic political forces of the twentieth century, no matter how divergent they appear on the surface, are really tending in the same direction, that of the new world state. . . . All are

in the same direction, that of the new world state. . . . All are fundamentally materialist. . . . They all glorify machines and modern technology. They all . . . subordinate the individual to the claims of a collective whole. . . . Moreover, aside from these general resemblances, there seem to be quite specific links between each one of these political systems of the twentieth century and the new world state: from fascism comes the caste system; from communism, the emphasis on conditioning and propaganda; and from democratic capitalism the economy oriented toward lavish and purposeless production and consumption. (1984, 83–84)

LITERATURE AND LANGUAGE WITHOUT MEANING

Beneath the irony of Huxley's naming lies a society whose literature and language are almost completely devoid of real meaning. Words still exist, but the concepts for which they stand have been altered. *Love* no longer connotes an emotional bond, only sexual activity; *conventionality* equals *promiscuity;* calling a woman *pneumatic* is a compliment rather than an insult; and *stability* means a society in which infantilism is not only encouraged, but enforced. Characters speak, but the import of what they say escapes them:

> What happens to the meaning of *normality* when Mr. Foster explains he wants to give the Epsilon embryo "the normality of dogs and cows"? . . . From chapter to chapter the destruction of the meaning of words proceeds apace. Foster explains that childhood has been abolished because the years between an Epsilon's birth and the time he is fit for work constitute a "superfluous and wasted immaturity." Yet the Epsilon's so-called maturity is scarcely that of a five-year-old. Surely this is no great improvement on the treatment of children in nineteenth-century England. (Meckier 1969, 181–82)

Huxley repeatedly refers to items that substitute for other things: "blood-surrogate," "morocco-surrogate," "Pregnancy Substitute," "oboe-surrogate," "Violent Passion Surrogate," "vitaminized beef-surrogate." New words refer to things that have been altered, ostensibly for the better, with the originals no longer in evidence: "hyper-violin," "super-cornet," "pan-glandular biscuits," "super-doves." Some things seem familiar enough but have been renamed, and their strangeness makes us wonder if they are, in fact, the same. Is "boiling caffeine solution" a cup of tea, coffee—or what? When an infant finishes sucking a pint of "pasteurized external secretion," is it cows' milk, human milk, goats' milk—or is it milk

ture") somehow different from a talking Feely? Since the characters take these things for granted, the questions are not answered within the narrative. Language and meaning diverge, as the artificial stability of the World State depends on arresting the population's development. . . .

A TERRIFYING VISION

Persuasively, Meckier notes that "the new society's use of language is one long and recurrent illustration of how life has not gained in meaning but become instead absolutely meaningless" (1969, 179). Of all the futuristic visions Huxley presents in *Brave New World*, it is his depiction of a language that has been almost completely stripped of real meaning that is most terrifying. Huxley's emphasis fixes language issues as central for all subsequent dystopias, even though comparatively few dystopian writers have concurred with his premise of a society whose emphasis is on control through happiness. *Nineteen Eighty-four*, the next major dystopian novel of the century, consciously broke with almost all Huxley's dystopian visions—yet it continued to foreground the issues of language in a dystopian society, and even more overtly so than Huxley did in *Brave New World*. Where Huxley portrays a society that has impoverished language by suppressing meaning, George Orwell paints a grim picture of one that suppresses language in order to destroy meaning. *Brave New World* posits islands on which the misfits can express their individuality freely, in language and literature. But in *Nineteen Eighty-four*'s Oceania, there are no such isles of the blessed, even within the minds of misfits and rebels—indeed, especially not there.

SELECTED BIBLIOGRAPHY

Aldiss, Brian, and David Wingrove. *Trillion Year Spree: The History of Science Fiction*. New York: Atheneum, 1986. Reprint and revision of *Billion Year Spree*. London: Weidenfeld and Nicholson, 1973.

Baker, Robert S. *Brave New World: History, Science and Dystopia*. Twayne's Masterwork Studies, no. 39. Boston: Twayne Publishers, 1990.

Bradford, Gamaliel. *The Quick and the Dead*. Boston: Houghton-Mifflin, 1931.

Firchow, Peter Edgerly. *The End of Utopia: A Study of Aldous Huxley's* Brave New World. Lewisburg, PA: Bucknell University Press, 1984.

Kumar, Krishan. *Utopia and Anti-Utopia in Modern Times.* Oxford, UK: Basil Blackwell, 1987.

Matter, William. "On *Brave New World.*" In *No Place Else: Explorations in Utopian and Dystopian Fiction,* ed. Eric S. Rabkin, Martin H. Greenberg, and Joseph D. Olander, 94–109. Carbondale: Southern Illinois University Press, 1983.

Meckier, Jerome. *Aldous Huxley: Satire and Structure.* London: Chatto and Windus, 1969.

Wells, H[erbert] G[eorge]. *Men like Gods.* New York: Macmillan, 1923.

———. *The Works of H.G. Wells,* Vol. 2. Atlantic Edition. [Contains *The Island of Doctor Moreau* and *The Sleeper Awakes.*] London: T. Fisher Unwin, 1924.

Huxley's Manuscript Revisions

Donald Watt

Most of Huxley's original manuscripts have been lost
or destroyed, reports Donald Watt. Fortunately, a version of *Brave New World* with many of the author's
additions and emendations has survived. By examining Huxley's manuscript changes, Watt is able to trace
the development of the story as well as the author's attempts to flesh out his characters. Watt is the editor of
Aldous Huxley: The Critical Heritage.

For Aldous Huxley, the late spring and summer of 1931 was
a period of challenging creative activity. On 18 May he wrote
Mrs. Kethevan Roberts that he was composing a novel about
the future, "on the horror of the Wellsian Utopia and a revolt
against it." He confided that he was finding the task "very difficult," and he expressed concern over his ability to manage
it: "I have hardly enough imagination to deal with such a
subject."[1] Nine days later Huxley felt compelled to cancel a
trip to Russia with his brother, Julian, because of problems
with the composition of his book. Everything he had written
in the past month, he lamented, had to be rewritten "in quite
another way." He regarded the setback as a "literary cata-
strophe" which "throws me right back in my work" (*Letters,*
348–49). In a few weeks Huxley wrote Sidney Schiff (21 June
1931) about his deep involvement in his revisions: "I'm
working very hard, re-writing large chunks of what I had
thought definitively done and praying heaven that this time
the revision may be final—while before me lie great deserts
of the yet unwritten. So the Summer promises to be a well-

---

1. *Letters of Aldous Huxley*, ed. Grover Smith (London: Chatto and Windus, 1969), p.
348. Hereafter cited in text as *Letters*. Huxley said his novel "started out as a parody of
H.G. Wells's *Men Like Gods*, but gradually it got out of hand and turned into something
quite different from what I'd originally intended." See *Writers at Work: The "Paris Review" Interviews*, Second Series (New York: Viking, 1963), p. 198.

From Donald Watt, "The Manuscript Revisions of *Brave New World*," *Journal of English
and German Philology*, vol. 77 (1978), pp. 367–82. Copyright 1978 by the Board of Trustees
of the University of Illinois. Used with the permission of the University of Illinois Press.

occupied time."[2] Almost three months after his reluctant renunciation of the Russian venture with Julian, Huxley apologized to his father for a "shockingly long" hiatus in their correspondence: "My only excuse is that I have been harried with work—which I have at last, thank heaven, got rid of:—a comic, or at least satirical, novel about the Future." The sigh of relief in Huxley's letter is almost audible: "It has been a job writing the book and I'm glad it's done" (*Letters*, 351).

The cause of all the turmoil, and what occupied Huxley during those intervening three months, was of course the preparation of *Brave New World*.

Such labor in the composition of a novel was not unusual for Huxley. He told an interviewer toward the end of his life: "Generally, I write everything many times over. All my thoughts are second thoughts. And I correct each page a great deal, or rewrite it several times as I go along."[3] What is unusual is that, in the case of *Brave New World*, the manuscript of the novel is extant. A fire which in 1961 ruined Huxley's home in California also destroyed most of the manuscripts of his works, including *Antic Hay* and *Point Counter Point*.[4] It seems reasonable to conclude that the *Brave New World* script is probably the only surviving record of how Huxley composed his major fiction. The study of this script therefore yields some rare insights into the Huxleyan creative process in action.

A glance at the script confirms the impression of high challenge and laborious pursuit that Huxley gives in his correspondence on the composition of the novel. *Brave New World* was born amid a tangle of lined-out phrases, typed-over words, rearranged passages, and tireless autograph [handwritten] insertions. . . .

VIVID DETAILS, PRECISELY CHOSEN

Huxley sought persistently in his script to create a vivid, concrete picture of his brave new world. A major concern of his revisions was to filter out vague generalities and to replace them with life-evoking specific details comprehensible within the context of such a future society as he describes. At the opening of "Three Weeks in a Helicopter," for example,

2. Clementine Robert, *Aldous Huxley, Exhumations: Correspondance inédite avec Sydney Schiff (1925–1937)* (Paris: Didier, 1976), p. 73. 3. *Writers at Work*, p. 197. 4. Sybille Bedford, *Aldous Huxley: A Biography, Volume Two: 1939–1963* (London: Chatto and Windus, 1974), pp. 278–79.

the gigantic black in Huxley's script at first embraces a mere "golden-haired young girl." In Huxley's revision she becomes "a golden-haired brachycephalic Beta plus female" (TS, 158/CW, 198).[5] In describing "the famous British Museum Massacre" toward the close of Chapter III, Huxley originally had the unfortunate two thousand culture fans "squashed by tanks." In the revision it seemed more fitting to have them "gassed with dichlorethyl sulfide" (TS, 56/CW, 58). At the Amsterdam wrestling match in Chapter VI, Lenina in the script at first presses only *soma* upon Bernard. In a revision the *soma* turns into a "half-gramme raspberry sundae" (TS, 84/CW, 104). Lenina originally recalls Fanny's account of Bernard's unorthodoxy: "According to Fanny, Bernard was badly conditioned." This is given more point in the revision: "'Alcohol in his blood surrogate,' was Fanny's explanation of every eccentricity" (TS, 83/CW, 102). . . .

A special way in which Huxley sharpened the verisimilitude of his tale was by inserting and improving upon pieces of hypnopaedic wisdom. When Lenina tries in Chapter VI to calm Bernard, Huxley at first wrote: "'Don't lose your temper,' she said, while repeating her nocturnal lessons; 'take *soma* instead.'" But Huxley later lined out the words following "she said" and inserted: "'Remember, one cubic centimetre cures ten gloomy sentiments'" (TS, 85/CW, 104). The hypnopaedic slogans are concrete emblems of the sense and the style of Huxley's Fordian future. One of Huxley's happiest changes in script, in fact, was the improvement of the flat "When a man feels, the state reels" to the melodic "When the individual feels the community reels" (TS, 88/CW, 109).

As conscientious as he was in working credible details into his presentation of the new world, Huxley knew he had to guard against excessiveness and tiresome exposition. For example, from Foster's account of the embryos' progress Huxley crossed out two-thirds of a script page dealing with bottle-labelling and the details of the Social Predestinators' tasks (TS, 10/CW, 10). A little later he cut out over half a page explaining the need for Epsilons as well as Alphas (TS, 16/CW, 15–16). Huxley must have realized his narrative could easily find itself bogged down in too much explicit de-

---

5. CW refers to the Chatto and Windus first edition of *Brave New World* published in London in 1932; TS refers to the typescript.

scription. Sufficient details were required for creating a sense of authenticity, but in many cases evocative, not explicit details were judged to be most effective. The children's games at the beginning of Chapter III, for instance, were introduced in the typescript quite literally: "The ball games were very elaborate, requiring They [*sic*] could only be played with the aid of a great deal of rather complicated apparatus." In Huxley's hand, though, this was deleted from the opening paragraph and replaced by a passage describing the setting: "The roses were in bloom, two nightingales soliloquized in the boskage, a cuckoo was just going out of tune among the lime trees. The air was drowsy with the murmur of bees and helicopters" (TS 33/CW, 33). The unnatural union of those "bees and helicopters" does more for Huxley's narrative at this point then several pages of explanation. . . . Innuendo and concision, Huxley must have felt, were among the more effective ways of portraying the new world. . . .

The script suggests that Huxley's initial chore was to conceive and to assemble the complex vision of the future he saw threatening to evolve out of the present. His letter to Mrs. Roberts expresses his reservations about his ability to accomplish the task. Simply to articulate that vision seems to have occupied the bulk of Huxley's attention as he wrote his first working draft. His attitude toward the new world, though, reflected through the satirical tone of the authorial voice, was the result of considerable pruning and shaping. Much of the book's irony was injected into Huxley's script during the process of revision.

There are a number of autograph insertions in the script that show Huxley in the act of adjusting the finer ironical tones of his narrative. For example, after the Solidarity Service of Chapter V has been consummated, Huxley at first described Fifi Bradlaugh's state of rapture as "the rich peace of balanced life, of energies at rest and in equilibrium." This was revised in hand to present Miss Bradlaugh's contentment as one "of balanced life, of energies at rest and in equilibrium. A rich and living peace" (TS, 82/ CW, 99). The change in emphasis is delicate, but the intensified irony of the added fragment is unmistakable. Similarly, when the Director begins his account of Bokanovsky's Process in Chapter I, Huxley wrote: "Making ninety-six human beings grow where only one grew before. [Illegible], for, paradoxically enough, the stimulus to do so is a negative stimulus." Huxley in a revision deleted the last sentence and inserted in hand the single damning word, "Progress" (TS, 5/CW, 5). . . . One wonders, in view of the care Huxley took internally to express his dismay with Fordian London, how so many of his book's early reviewers could have thought he was advocating its view of the future.[6]

PROBLEMS IN BRINGING CHARACTERS TO LIFE

Verisimilitude in the construction of details, concise and emphatic styling, and the creation of an ironic tone were refinements that Huxley in his vintage years as a novelist was well equipped to accomplish as he revised *Brave New World.* Characterization, on the other hand, was another question. In his *Paris Review* interview Huxley conceded: "I'm not very good at creating people; I don't have a very wide repertory of characters."[7] The revisions of *Brave New World* illustrate the sorts of problems Huxley encountered as he sought to give life to some of his main characters. Moreover, one can trace in Huxley's revisions of his three leading male characters the evolution of his novel's larger meaning. Huxley's script suggests that he thought first of making Bernard an orthodox rebel against his society, and then, instead, of making John a potentially redeeming noble savage hero brought into that society from the outside. But the progress of the revisions shows Huxley painstakingly rejecting both options to create the collapsing structural ironies to which he alludes in his 1946 Foreword to the book.[8]

The revisions dealing with the molding of Bernard Marx's character are among the most extensive in the script. Huxley's readily acknowledged difficulties in character creation are at once illustrated and complicated by the manuscript changes he makes in Bernard's role in the novel. That Huxley was not sure enough of his drawing of Bernard can be seen in revisions which show him inserting statements of what the narrative amply dramatizes. When he alluded to

6. See *Aldous Huxley: The Critical Heritage,* ed. Donald Watt (London: Routledge and Kegan Paul, 1975), pp. 197–222. Two recent source studies by Peter Firchow are of considerable help in understanding the complex influences Huxley brought to his novel: "Science and Conscience in Huxley's *Brave New World,*" *Contemporary Literature,* 16 (Summer 1975), 301–16; and "Wells and Lawrence in Huxley's *Brave New World,*" *Journal of Modern Literature,* 5 (April 1976), 260–78. 7. *Writers at Work,* p. 206. 8. "At the time the book was written this idea, that human beings are given free will in order to choose between insanity on the one hand and lunacy on the other, was one that I found amusing and regarded as quite possibly true." "Foreword," *Brave New World* (New York: Modern Library, 1946), p. [vi].

the practical jokes other Alpha men play upon Bernard owing to his substandard physique, Huxley felt obliged to elaborate in autograph: "The mockery made him feel an outsider; and feeling an outsider he behaved like one, which increased the prejudice against him and intensified the contempt and hostility aroused by his physical defects. Which in turn increased his sense of being alien and alone" (TS, 68/CW, 76). A page or two later, as Huxley developed the contrast between Bernard and Helmholtz, he inserted in hand: "What the two men shared was the knowledge that they were individuals" (TS, 70/CW, 79). Such additions are unnecessary, if not intrusive. The point is that in his uncertainty Huxley goes against the grain of his other revisions, which sustainedly guard against too much explicitness.

Huxley must have wrestled with the creation of Bernard's character all the way to the publisher. There are some pertinent materials missing from the extant typescript which nonetheless appear in the first edition, evidently as a result of last-minute revisions by Huxley. For example, the final two paragraphs of the middle section of Chapter VI, where Bernard gives Helmholtz a boastful and exaggerated report of his encounter with the Director, are not in the typescript. This is important, because without those two paragraphs Bernard leaves the Director, after receiving a reprimand for his unorthodoxy, on a modestly positive note: "Iceland was just a threat. A most stimulating and life-giving threat. Walking along the corridor, he actually whistled" (TS, 93/CW, 115). But the added paragraphs remove any trace of real assertiveness from Bernard and stress the hypocrisy of his character. Another late addition to Huxley's portrait of Bernard occurs in Chapter II, as Lenina explains to Fanny why she thinks Bernard's smallness is attractive: "One feels one would like to pet him. You know. Like a cat" (CW, 53). This remark is not in the extant typescript. Huxley must have wished in his last revisions to prepare his reader early in the story for Bernard's essential domestication.

Amid Huxley's struggles to flesh out Bernard's character, one can discern in the script the progress of his thoughts about what Bernard would mean in the book. Huxley's initial conception of Bernard's role changed significantly during the course of his revisions. Alterations in the script suggest Huxley at first thought of Bernard as the novels hero, then switched to John as more fitting for the hero's role, and finally decided that Helmholtz, if anyone, should be the book's only authentically uplifting character. . . .

Traces of genuine rebellion and integrity in Bernard turned, in Huxley's emergent characterization, to presumptuousness and egotism. Huxley stressed Bernard's pompous behavior, his inflated sense of self-importance, in Chapter IX as Bernard informs the New Mexico warden of his telephone conversation with Mond. Huxley in autograph expanded his description of Bernard from "His tone was weary, bored" to "His bored tone implied that he was in the habit of talking to his fordship every day of the week" (TS, 134/CW, 168). . . .

Huxley at one point must have entertained a more heroic presentation of John's revolt against Fordian London. In a passage in the typescript which is absent from the first edition (at the close of Chapter XIV), after the khaki twin asks John if Linda is dead, Huxley wrote: "In the Savage's mind it was as though a sheet of opaque glass were suddenly and violently broken. There was light. He saw in an instant what he must do." But Huxley replaced this in the published novel with: "The Savage stared at them for a moment in silence" (TS, 199/CW, 245). Further, at the very end of the dialogue between John and Mustapha Mond in Chapter XVII, Huxley typed and then crossed out the following after Mond shrugs his shoulders: "'You won't find many other claimants,' [he?] said. 'That's where I believe you're wrong,' said the Savage" (TS, 230). One is led to suspect that Huxley had a more crusading reading of John in mind at some stage in the writing. . . .

Of the three incipient rebels, the only one who escaped Huxley's sobering modifications as he revised his script was Helmholtz. Helmholtz's character is largely unrealized, surely neglected and underdeveloped. But Huxley did make a pair of autograph revisions of some significance for Helmholtz's role in the book. Huxley emphasized Helmholtz's natural kindness and his genuine personal quality by stressing the contrast between him and Bernard in Chapter XII, where Helmholtz generously overlooks Bernard's neglect and revives their friendship. Huxley added in hand to his script: "Touched, Bernard at the same time felt himself humiliated by the magnanimity, which was the more extraordinary and therefore the more humiliating for him in that it owed nothing to *soma*: it was the Helmholtz of daily life who forgave and forgot, not the Helmholtz of a half-gramme holiday" (TS, 171/CW, 212). A page later Huxley added a key paragraph concerning Helmholtz's creative instincts: "Helmholtz only laughed. 'I feel,' he said after a silence, 'as though I were beginning to have something to say. As though I were beginning to be able to use that power inside me— that extra latent power. Something seems to be coming. . . .' In a strange way he seemed profoundly happy" (TS, 172). With minor emendations this would find its way into the published novel (CW, 214). It is perhaps instructive to note, too, that earlier in the script Bernard refers to "poor little Helmholtz Watson" (TS, 97), that the adjectives are subsequently deleted, and that, accordingly, the two characters may have reversed roles in Huxley's mind as he labored over his story. At the least, Huxley must have envisioned Helmholtz adopting a more positive role as the characters of Bernard and John were undergoing revision .

Discovering What He Really Wanted to Say

What all this means, I believe, is that as Huxley approached the climax of his book he was still working out the identities and relationships of his main characters. Evidence in the script suggests that Huxley also must have had important second thoughts about the novel's concluding chapters. At a comparatively late stage of the composition, Huxley rearranged his script to enliven what threatened to become a dull confrontation scene and to add greater clarity and force to his presentation of the Savage. Most important, Huxley interjected the Park Lane Hospital sequences (Chapters XIV–XV) between Lenina's abortive seduction of John and John's appearance before Mustapha Mond. The Park Lane Hospital additions bring Huxley's trio of rebels into open defiance of their society. By this significant move, Huxley discovered at once a means of adding substantial drama to his narrative's crisis point and a way of lending greater credibility to his final presentation of John's motivations. Huxley's revisions of his last chapters thereby show him fusing what he finally wished to say in the book with the most effective way of saying it. . . .

Besides diversifying his characters and dramatizing the action, Huxley in his revisions was in the act of discovering what he really wanted to say in *Brave New World*. The old world of noble savagery from which Huxley's friend, D.H. Lawrence, derived meaning was, Huxley was now coming to see, dead.[9] The impulse which caused Huxley at first to think of John as his hero was perhaps one of the last effects of Lawrence's influence upon him. On the other hand, the new world of H.G. Wells was not at all powerless to be born. It is significant that Huxley's revisions of Bernard show him not as an authentic rebel against dystopia, but as one whose discontent derives mainly from his desire to be accepted in such a society. Huxley in the early 1930s was beginning to believe that man's hope for any authentic existence lay beyond these two worlds.

9. See Jerome Meckier, "Huxley's Lawrencian Interlude: The 'Latin Compromise' That Failed," *Aldous Huxley: Satire and Structure* (London: Chatto and Windus, 1969), pp. 78–123.

Huxley's Characters Are Appropriate for the Novel

Peter Edgerly Firchow

One of the leading Huxley scholars, Peter Edgerly Firchow, takes issue with Donald Watt over the question of Huxley's characters. Watt, agreeing with Huxley himself, suggested that creating characters was not the author's strong point. But Firchow notes that it is appropriate for most of the characters in a world that shuns individuality to be rather flat; moreover, he asserts, the characters are more complex than most people recognize. Firchow is the author of *Aldous Huxley: Satirist and Novelist.*

If there are plenty of good scientific and technological reasons—ectogenesis, cloning, serial mass production, TV—why *Brave New World* could not have been written before it was, there are also some very good literary reasons. For *Brave New World* is, literarily speaking, a very modern book; modern not only because it deals frankly with a typically "modern" subject like sex, but modern in the very ways it conceives of and presents its subject and characters.

There are in *Brave New World* no long introductory descriptions of landscape or environment in the Victorian or Edwardian manner; there is, initially, no attempt to give more than a very rudimentary outline of the physical and psychological traits of the characters. There is no elaborate explanation of how we came to be where we are, nor even at first an explanation at all why we are where we are: six-hundred-odd years in the future. The starting assumption is simply that it is quite normal to be in a big factory in the middle of London. Only gradually and indirectly does that assumption also become startling, as it becomes clear to us

Excerpted from Peter Edgerly Firchow, *The End of Utopia: A Study of Aldous Huxley's "Brave New World"* (Lewisburg, PA: Bucknell University Press, 1984). Copyright © 1984 by Associated Presses, Inc. Reprinted with permission.

what the products of this factory are and what kind of a world we have entered.

This technique of indirection is one that Virginia Woolf ascribes, in "Mr. Bennett and Mrs. Brown" (1924), to the moderns. For her—and by extension for the modern novelist—the way to get at the heart of a character and a situation is not to add up every item of information we can gather about them; the whole is not to be found in the summing up of all of the parts. That way lies dullness—and Arnold Bennett. The better way is to try to get at the whole by being, as it were, paradoxically content with the part. To get at the essence of Mrs. Brown—Woolf's hypothetical example—we need to be told nothing directly of her history and background; we merely need to overhear her conversation in a railway compartment for an hour or so. Out of the apparently random odds and ends of this conversation, we can, by an act of the imagination, reconstruct her life and penetrate her soul. . . .

INDIRECTION AND COUNTERPOINT

The first three chapters of *Brave New World*, especially, are masterfully composed in the indirect manner. Very little is heard; almost everything is overheard. To this manner Huxley also adds a refinement of his own devising, a technique perhaps best called "counterpoint," since Huxley had used it most fully before in *Point Counter Point* (1929), though there are intimations of it as early as *Those Barren Leaves* (1925). This technique involves a simultaneous juxtaposition of different elements of the narrative, much as musical counterpoint means sounding different notes simultaneously with a *cantus firmus.* The result in music is—or should be—a complex harmony; in Huxley's fiction the result is, usually, a complex dissonance, a subtle and often brilliant cacophony of ironies. The third chapter of *Brave New World* is set up entirely in this kind of counterpoint, gathering together the various narrative strains of the first two chapters and juxtaposing them without any editorial comment, slowly at first and then with gathering momentum, climaxing in a crescendo that fuses snatches of Mond's lecture, Lenina's conversation with Fanny, Henry Foster's with Benito Hoover, Bernard Marx's resentful thoughts, and bits of hypnopaedic wisdom.

The result is astonishing and far more effective in drawing us into the noisy and frantically joyless atmosphere of the new world state than pages of descriptive writing would have been. It is one of the most remarkable pieces of writing in the modern British novel.

Brave New World is modern, too, in another literary respect. It is shot through with literary allusions. Most of these allusions—such as the title and much of the conversation of the Savage—are to Shakespeare, but there are also more or less direct or indirect allusions to Shaw, Wells, T.S. Eliot, D.H. Lawrence, Voltaire, Rousseau, Thomas Gray, and Dante. The point of these allusions is not, I think, to show how clever and sophisticated and knowledgeable a writer Aldous Huxley is; the point is, rather, as in the poetry of T.S. Eliot—or Huxley's own poetry, for that matter—to reveal ironically the inadequacies of the present (or the present as contained in the future) by comparing it with the past. This is primarily how the literary allusions function in *The Waste Land* or in "Whispers of Immortality"—from which Huxley derives Lenina's peculiarly pneumatic sexuality—and that is also how they function primarily in *Brave New World*.[1] The juxtaposition of Cleopatra with a bored modern woman who has nothing to do or of Spenser's and Goldsmith's lovers with the dreary amorous adventures of a modern secretary serves the same purpose as the juxtaposition of the love of Othello and Desdemona with that of the hero and heroine of the "feely" "Three Weeks in a Helicopter," or even the love of Romeo and Juliet with that of Lenina and the Savage. The effect in both cases is that of a literary double exposure, which provides a simultaneous view of two quite distinct and yet horribly similar realities. The tension between the two—that which pulls them violently apart and at the same time pushes them violently together—produces a powerful irony, which is just what Eliot and Huxley want to produce. By means of this irony it then becomes possible for Huxley, or the "narrator" of his novel, to guide the reader's response without seeming to do so, without requiring any overt interference on his part. By merely hinting, for example, at the analogy between the Fordian state and Prospero's island, Huxley manages to convey ironically a disapproval of that state without ever having to voice it himself. And he can

---

1. But if *Brave New World* is indebted to *The Waste Land*, as Grover Smith has pointed out in *T.S. Eliot's Poetry and Plays: A Study in Sources and Meaning* (Chicago: University of Chicago Press, 1956), p. 76, then Eliot owes Madame Sosostris to Huxley's *Crome Yellow*.

safely leave it to the reader to make the rest of the ironic identification; Mond is Prospero; Lenina is Miranda; the Savage is Ferdinand; Bernard Marx is Caliban. Or, if one prefers, Mond is a kind of Prospero and Alonso combined; the Savage, as befits his name, is Caliban, and his mother, Linda, is Sycorax; Lenina is a perverse Miranda and Bernard a strange Ferdinand. Or, to give another twist to it, the Director of Hatcheries and Conditioning is a kind of Alonso who abandoned Linda and John to the desert; they in turn are, respectively, Prospero and Miranda, with their sexes reversed; the Indians and especially Popé are a kind of collective Caliban; Lenina, the aggressive lover, is a female Ferdinand, and Bernard a sort of rescuing Ariel. The same kind of ironic game can be played with *Romeo and Juliet* and *Othello.* In this way the ironies multiply until they become mind-boggling.[2]

This is not to say that there is no direct narrative guidance in Huxley's novel. The reader is explicitly told, for example, that mental excess has produced in Helmholtz Watson's character the same results as a physical defect has in Bernard Marx. Or Bernard's psyche is analyzed for us in terms of an inferiority complex that finds its chief victims in his friends rather than his enemies. These are all acts of narrative interference and by no means isolated ones, but even so they are kept in the background and are, generally speaking, confined to attempts to make the psychological functioning of the characters more comprehensible.

Brave New World is a novel that is very carefully planned and put together. As Donald Watt has recently shown in his study of Huxley's revisions in the typescript of *Brave New World,* a number of the best stylistic effects and one of the best scenes—the soma distribution riot—were afterthoughts, inserted by Huxley after he had finished the rest of the novel.[3] . . .

2. For studies of Huxley's use of Shakespeare in *Brave New World,* see R.H. Wilson, "*Brave New World* as Shakespeare Criticism," *The Shakespeare Association Bulletin* 21 (July 1946): 99–107; Jerome Meckier, "Shakespeare and Aldous Huxley," *Shakespeare Quarterly* 22 (Spring 1971): 129–35; and J.A.A. Powell, "The Vanishing Values—Huxley's Permutations of *The Tempest,*" Ph.D. diss., University of Utah, 1973. Some of Huxley's allusions are not literary at all but purely personal and even whimsical, as for instance the description of Eton College, which Huxley had attended himself and where he had taught at the end of the first World War. Miss Keate, the headmistress, derives her name from John Keate (1773–1852), an Eton headmaster who was infamous for the scale and severity of his beatings. So too the "Aphroditeum" alludes to the Athenaeum, an elite London club to which Huxley belonged and where he often stayed while visiting London. 3. Donald Watt, "The Manuscript Revisions of *Brave New World,*" *Journal of English and Germanic Philology* 77 (July 1978): 380.

REWRITING CHARACTERS

One of the chief problems Huxley had with *Brave New World,* according to Donald Watt, was with the characters. On the evidence of the revisions, Watt concludes that Huxley seems first to have thought of making Bernard Marx the rebellious hero of the novel but then changed his mind and deliberately played him down into a kind of anti-hero. After rejecting the possibility of a heroic Bernard, Huxley next seems to have turned to the Savage as an alternative. According to Watt, there are in the typescript several indications, later revised or omitted, of the Savage's putting up or at least planning to put up violent resistance to the new world state, perhaps even of leading a kind of revolution against it. But in the process of rewriting the novel, Huxley also abandoned this idea in favor of having no hero at all, or of having only the vague adumbration of a hero in Helmholtz Watson.[4]

Watt's analysis of the revisions in *Brave New World* is very helpful and interesting; he shows convincingly, I think, that Huxley was unable to make up his mind until very late in the composition of the novel just what direction he wanted the story and the leading male characters to take. From this uncertainty, however, I do not think it necessary to leap to the further conclusion that Huxley had difficulty in creating these characters themselves. Huxley's supposedly inadequate ability to create living characters, the result of his not being a "congenital novelist," is a question that often arises in discussions of his fiction, and in connection with longer and more traditionally novelistic novels like *Point Counter Point* or *Eyeless in Gaza* (1936) appropriately so. But *Brave New World* is anything but a traditional novel in this sense. It is not a novel of character but a relatively short satirical tale, a "fable," much like Voltaire's *Candide.* One hardly demands fully developed and "round" characters of *Candide,* nor should one of *Brave New World.*

THE CHARACTERS ARE ENTIRELY APPROPRIATE

This is all the more the case because the very nature of the new world state precludes the existence of fully developed characters. Juliets and Anna Kareninas, or Hamlets and

4. Watt, "Manuscript," pp. 374, 377.

Prince Vronskys, are by definition impossibilities in the new world state. To ask for them is to ask for a different world, the very world whose absence Huxley's novel so savagely laments. Character, after all, is shaped by suffering, and the new world state has abolished suffering in favor of a continuous, soma-stupefied, infantile "happiness." In such an environment it is difficult to have characters who grow and develop and are "alive."

Despite all this, it is surprising and noteworthy how vivid and even varied Huxley's characters are. With all their uniformly standardized conditioning, Alphas and Betas turn out to be by no means alike: the ambitious "go-getter" Henry Foster is different from his easy-going friend Benito Hoover; the unconventional and more "pneumatic" Lenina Crowne from the moralistic and rather less pneumatic Fanny Crowne; the resentful and ugly Bernard Marx from the handsome and intelligent Helmholtz Watson. Huxley, in fact, seems to work consistently and consciously in terms of contrastive/complementary pairs to suggest various possibilities of response to similar situations. So, too, Helmholtz and the Savage are another pair, as are the Savage and Mond, Mond and the DHC, Bernard and Henry Foster. The most fully developed instance of this pairing or doubling technique is the trip that Bernard and Lenina make to the Indian reservation, a trip that duplicates the one made some years earlier by the DHC and a "particularly pneumatic" Beta-Minus named Linda. Like the DHC, Bernard also leaves Lenina, another pneumatic Beta, (briefly) behind while returning to civilization, and during this interval she, too, is lusted after by a savage, much as Popé and the other Indians lust after Linda. Even the novel as a whole reveals a similar sort of doubling structure, with the new world state on the one hand and the Indian reservation on the other.

Within limits, the characters, even some of the minor and superficial characters like Henry Foster, are capable of revealing other and deeper facets of their personality. Returning with Lenina from the Stoke Poges Obstacle Golf Course, Henry Foster's helicopter suddenly shoots upward on a column of hot air rising from the Slough Crematorium.[5] Lenina

---

5. The mention of Stoke Poges is probably intended to evoke in the reader's mind the "Elegy Written in a Country Churchyard," whose author lies buried there. For another and fuller parodic allusion to the same poem, see Malinda Snow, "The Gray Parody in *Brave New World*," *Papers on Language and Literature* 13 (Winter 1977): 85.

is delighted at this brief switchback, but "Henry's tone was almost, for a moment, melancholy. 'Do you know what that switchback was?' he said. 'It was some human being finally and definitely disappearing. Going up in a squirt of hot gas. It would be curious to know who it was—a man or a woman, an Alpha or an Epsilon . . .'" Henry quickly jolts himself out of this atypical mood and reverts to his normally obnoxious cheerfulness, but for an instant at least there was a glimpse of a real human being.

Much more than Henry, Bernard Marx and Helmholtz Watson are capable of complexity of response. The latter especially and partly through his contact with the Savage grows increasingly aware of himself as a separate human entity and of his dissatisfaction with the kind of life he had led hitherto. As an Emotional Engineer and contriver of slogans, Helmholtz has been very successful, as he also has been in the capacities of lover and sportsman; but he despises this success and seeks for a satisfaction for which he has no name and which he can only dimly conceive. He comes closest to expressing it in the poem that eventually leads to his exile, the poem in which an ideal and absent woman becomes more real to him—in the manner of Mallarmé's flower that is absent from all bouquets—than any woman he has ever actually met.

In the end Helmholtz agrees to being sent into frigid exile in the Falkland Islands. The reason he chooses such a place rather than possible alternatives like Samoa or the Marquesas is because there he will not only have solitude but also a harsh climate in which to suffer and to gain new and very different experiences. His aim, however, is not, as some critics have suggested, to seek mystic experience;[6] he simply wants to learn how to write better poetry. "I should like a thoroughly bad climate," he tells Mustapha Mond. "I believe one would write better if the climate were bad. If there were a lot of wind and storms for example . . ." This hardly represents a search for mysticism and God; in this novel only the Savage, and he in only a very qualified way, can be described as seeking after such ends. Helmholtz merely wants more and better words. . . .

---

6. Notably Jerome Meckier in "A Neglected Huxley 'Preface': His Earliest Synopsis of *Brave New World*," *Twentieth Century Literature*, 25 (Spring 1979), 7–8, but also Watt, "Manuscript," 375.

THE IMPORTANCE OF BERNARD MARX

The same is true of Bernard Marx. Despite the apparent fact that Huxley once had more exalted intentions for him, Bernard belongs very much to the familiar Huxleyan category of the anti-hero, best exemplified perhaps by Theodore Gumbril, Jr., the so-called Complete Man of *Antic Hay* (1923). Like Gumbril, Bernard is able to envision and even seek after a love that is not merely sexual, but, like Gumbril again, his search is half-hearted. He is willing to settle for less because it is so much easier than trying to strive for more. Bernard is weak and cowardly and vain, much more so than Gumbril, and this makes him an unsympathetic character in a way that Gumbril is not. Nevertheless Bernard is undoubtedly capable of seeing the better, even if in the end he follows the worse.

Bernard is certainly a more fully developed character than Helmholtz; he is, in fact, with the exception of the Savage, the character about whom we know most in the entire novel. Just why this should be so is a question worth asking, just as it is worth asking why Bernard is the first of the novel's three malcontents to be brought to our attention.[7]

Bernard's importance resides, I think, in his incapacity. The stability of the new world state can be threatened, it is clear, from above and from below. In the case of Helmholtz the threat is from above, from a surfeit of capacity; in Bernard's case it is from below, from a lack of sufficient capacity. This is not simply to say that Bernard is more stupid than Helmholtz, which he probably is, but rather that because of his physical inferiority he has developed a compulsive need to assert his superiority. It is this incapacity which, paradoxically, seems to make Bernard the more dangerous threat, for it compels him to rise to a position of power in his society; he wants to be accepted by his society, but only on his own terms, terms that are not acceptable in the long run if stability is to be maintained. Helmholtz, on the other hand, is a loner who really wants to have nothing to do with the society at all, and in this sense he represents much less of a threat. The Savage, on the other hand, though most violent

7. According to Theodor W. Adorno's "Aldous Huxley und die Utopie" (1942; 1951), Bernard Marx is "a skeptically sympathetic caricature of a Jew." (my translation). This idea, aside from being absurd in itself in the context of *in vitro* generation, fails to take into account that Huxley had earlier portrayed non-Jewish characters with remarkably similar traits, such as Illidge in *Point Counter Point.* See the reprint of this essay in Adorno's *Prismen* (Berlin: Suhrkamp, [1955]), p. 127.

and uncompromising in his hatred of and desire to destroy the new world state, is really no threat at all, for he originates from outside the society. . . . There is never likely to be another Savage, but it is very probable that there will be or that there are more Bernards and Helmholtzes.

THE COMPLEXITY OF LENINA CROWNE

Both Bernard and Helmholtz are fairly complex characters. What is surprising, however, is that the same is true of Lenina Crowne. She seems at first to be nothing more than a pretty and addle-brained young woman without any emotional depth whatever. And at first it is true that this is all she is; but she changes in the course of the novel into something quite different. She changes because she falls in love.

The great irony of Lenina's falling in love is that she does not realize what it is that has happened to her; like Helmholtz she has no name for the new feeling and hence no way of conceiving or understanding what it is. She can only think of love in the physiological ways in which she has been conditioned to think of it; but her feeling is different.

So subtle is Huxley's portrayal of the change in Lenina that, as far as I know, no critic has ever commented on it. Yet Lenina is clearly predisposed from the very beginning to a love relationship that is not sanctioned by her society. As we learn from her conversation with Fanny, Lenina has been going with Henry Foster for four months without having had another man, and this in defiance of what she knows to be the properly promiscuous code of sexual behavior. When Fanny takes her up on this point of unconventionality, Lenina reacts almost truculently and replies that she "jolly well [does not] see why there should have been" anyone other than Henry. Her inability to see this error in her sexual ways is what predisposes her for the much greater and more intense feeling that she develops for the Savage.

The stages of her growing love for the Savage and her increasing mystification at what is happening within herself are handled with a brilliantly comic touch. There is the scene following Lenina's and the Savage's return from the feelies when the Savage sends her off in the taxicopter just as she is getting ready to seduce him. There is the touching moment when Lenina, who had once been terrified of pausing with Bernard to look at the sea and the moon over the Channel, now lingers "for a moment to look at the moon," before being summoned by an irritated and uncomprehending Arch-Songster. There is Lenina's increasing impatience with the obtuseness of Henry Foster and his blundering solicitousness. There are the fond murmurings to herself of the Savage's name. There is the conference with Fanny as to what she should do about the Savage's strange coldness toward her. There is her blunt rejection of Fanny's advice to seek consolation with one of the millions of other men. There is the wonderful scene in which she seeks out the Savage alone in his apartment, discovers to her amazement that he loves her, sheds her clothing, and receives, to her even greater amazement, insults, blows, and a threat to kill. There is the final terrible scene at the lighthouse when Lenina steps out of the helicopter, looks at the Savage with "an uncertain, imploring, almost abject smile," and then "pressed both hands to her left side [i.e., to her heart], and on that peach-bright, doll-beautiful face of hers appeared a strangely incongruous expression of yearning distress. Her blue eyes seemed to grow larger, brighter; and suddenly two tears rolled down her cheeks." Again the Savage attacks her, this time with his whip, maddened by desire, by remorse, and by the horde of obscenely curious sightseers. In the end, however, desire triumphs and the Savage and Lenina consummate their love in an orgy-porgian climax. When the Savage awakens to the memory of what has happened, he knows he cannot live with such defilement. For him the end is swift and tragic. For Lenina, however, there is no end; her tragedy—and for all the comedy and irony in which her love for the Savage is immersed, the word *tragedy* is not entirely inappropriate—her tragedy is that she has felt an emotion that she can never express or communicate or realize again.

PROFOUNDLY HUMAN CHARACTERS

The characters of *Brave New World*, it is safe to conclude, are not merely made of cardboard and *papier-mâché*. That they are nonetheless not full and complete human beings is quite true; but for all the technology and conditioning and impulses toward uniformity, there is still something profoundly human about them. As Lenina's development in the novel indicates, it is possible, as it were, to scratch the plasticized "doll-like" surface of a citizen—at least of an Alpha or Beta citizen—of the new world state and draw actual blood. In this sense and to this degree, Huxley's vision of the perfectly planned future is not without hope; for all the genetic engineering and conditioning, basic humanity remains much the same as it always was. Its imperfections and its needs, even under such greatly altered conditions, inevitably reappear. And it is for this reason, I think, that Huxley's vision is so extraordinarily powerful and compelling; because in the people he portrays we can still somehow recognize ourselves.

CHARACTERS AND PLOT

MAIN CHARACTERS

Tomakin—the Director of Hatcheries and Conditioning for Central London, also called the Director or D.H.C.

Henry Foster—an employee of the Hatchery, with a penchant for spouting statistics and a competitive spirit

Lenina Crowne—a pretty nurse who works in the Hatchery

Mustapha Mond—Resident Controller for Western Europe, one of the Ten World Controllers

Bernard Marx—an Alpha-Plus whose physical appearance was damaged as the result of a decanting accident; employed by the Psychology Bureau

Helmholtz Watson—a friend of Bernard's; an Alpha-Plus lecturer at the College of Emotional Engineering (Department of Writing) who might be, according to his superior, a little *too* able

John, the Savage—a young man who was born by accident, on the Savage Reservation

Linda—John's mother

PLOT

The novel opens with a tour of a cold, ugly building that serves as a hatchery and conditioning center in the world of A.F. 632. The Director of Hatcheries and Conditioning (D.H.C.) is explaining to students a little (as little as possible) about the work they will soon be doing as Fertilizers. People are now produced by machines on a factory production line, which produces sets of eight to ninety-six clones from a single egg. The cloning method, called Bokanovsky's Process, is "one of the major instruments of social stability," explains the D.H.C. Ovaries are harvested from women who are paid to undergo this sterilization. Then, using Podsnap's Technique to ripen all the eggs in an ovary at once and Bokanovsky's Process to clone each egg, the Hatchery is able to produce "nearly eleven thousand brothers and sisters in a hundred and fifty batches of identical twins, all within two years of the same age," he brags. An entire factory can be staffed with identical, standardized people, each doing exactly the same job.

At the behest of the director, Mr. Foster describes the embryos' journey from the Social Predestination Room to Decanting: the stage at which fertility ("merely a nuisance" in most cases) is suppressed, the predestining and conditioning of the embryos so they can be born ("decanted") fit for the place in society that has been ordained for them. Those destined for the lower castes are deprived of oxygen, so that those of the lowest caste, designated Epsilons, are little more than machines themselves, deprived of human intelligence. Other embryos are conditioned to hate the cold, so they will choose to work in the tropics; after decanting, they will be taught to love doing so. The Director explains, "That is the secret of happiness and virtue—liking what you've *got* to do. All conditioning aims at that: making people like their inescapable social destiny."

After briefly meeting a nurse, Lenina Crowne, who is working with the bottled embryos, the student tour next watches a Bokanovsky Group of eight-month-old Delta babies—the second-lowest caste—being conditioned by explosions and electric shock to hate flowers and books, so they would never wish to waste the Community's time on books, or on a love of nature, which, the D.H.C. explains, keeps no factories busy. He then shocks and embarrasses the students by referring to the old-time methods of producing children, when they were "born" to "parents." (He seems to enjoy forcing this "smut" on the students, in the name of science.) It was during those ancient days when the first principles of sleep-teaching, or hypnopaedia, were accidentally discovered, when some parents inadvertently allowed their son to sleep with a radio on all night. Now, hundreds of years later, sleep-teaching has been found useless in intellectual education, since "you can't learn a science unless you know what it's all about," but very useful in moral education, "which ought never, in any circumstances, to be rational." The students watch as Beta children taking an afternoon nap are given sleep lessons in Elementary Class Consciousness, having finished their Elementary Sex lessons for the day. The young sleepers are learning that they don't like children of other castes, who can be identified by the color of clothes they wear; they especially don't like to play with "stupid" Epsilons. On the other hand, they are (they are told) delighted to be Betas, who don't have to work as hard as the "frightfully clever" Alphas.

Outside, the students observe several hundred naked children playing in the sunshine. Rather than simple games, they are encouraged to use elaborate equipment designed to increase consumption, the D.H.C. explains. Children of seven or eight are engaged in rudimentary sex games; when one boy seems reluctant, he is hauled off to the Assistant Superintendent of Psychology to see if he is abnormal. The D.H.C. takes this opportunity to impart another historical tidbit: before the time of "Our Ford," and even for a while afterward, erotic play had been suppressed for people younger than twenty.

The history lesson is suddenly interrupted by the arrival of Mustapha Mond, one of the Ten World Controllers who make all the important decisions. He reminds the gathering of "Our Ford's" inspired saying, "History is bunk." Then, after promising the D.H.C. that he will not corrupt the students, he proceeds to describe for them the dreadful time when people lived with their "families." His description of the close quarters, intimacies, and emotions is so vivid that one student becomes ill. Our Ford—who for some unknown reason referred to himself as Our Freud when speaking of psychological matters—had been the first to reveal the misery and perversion, the appalling dangers of family life, monogamy, romance. The students protest with the words they have learned in sleep lessons: "But every one belongs to every one else." The Controller reminds the students how lucky they are that the old ways have been replaced with maximum stability: "No pains have been spared to make your lives emotionally easy—to preserve you, so far as that is possible, from having emotions at all."

Interspersed with the Controller's history lesson are scenes with Lenina Crowne, who has returned home after her work shift. She is talking with Fanny, whose locker is next to hers, about their evening plans. Lenina admits that she is going out again with Henry Foster, even though she has been dating him for four whole months and, worse, has not dated any other man during that time. When she says that she isn't very keen on promiscuity at times, Fanny urges her to get with the program, even if it takes an effort.

At the same time, Henry Foster is chatting with a coworker, the Assistant Predestinator, about Lenina. Henry says Lenina is "wonderfully pneumatic," and expresses surprise that this coworker hasn't had her yet. When the Assistant Predestinator promises to right that oversight soon, Bernard Marx, eavesdropping on their conversation, wants to attack the two of them for speaking of her as so much meat.

Meanwhile, Lenina is admitting that she is getting a bit bored with Henry Foster, and tells Peggy she is thinking of visiting a Savage Reservation with Bernard Marx. Peggy is shocked, since Bernard has a reputation for liking to spend time alone and dislikes Obstacle Golf, but Lenina responds that he is appealing because he is an Alpha-Plus, even if he is uncharacteristically small and ugly.

The Controller is telling the students about the wars to force people to consume; massacres of Simple Lifers, who wanted to get back to nature and consume fewer resources, and attacks on culture fans who wasted time in museums. But the Controllers decided force was not the answer, he reports; conditioning was a better way to destroy all that was disruptive from the old era, such as Shakespeare, Christianity, and alcohol. The tops were cut off the crosses to make T's, which would symbolize the new era: time as counted from the beginning of Our Ford's first T-Model, the prototypical product of the production line. Then, in A.F. 178, pharmacologists and bio-chemists were hired to create the perfect drug, soma, which would allow people to "take a holiday from reality whenever you like, and come back without so much as a headache or a mythology."

Henry Foster and the Assistant Predestinator, observing Bernard's foul mood, urge him to take soma. He refuses. Lenina meets Bernard on her way to a date with Henry for Obstacle Golf, and takes him up on his invitation to visit a Savage Reservation in July.

Bernard goes on to meet with his friend Helmholtz Watson. While Bernard feels separate from his fellows because of his physical differences, Helmholtz has begun to feel out of synch, too. He tells Bernard he feels as if he had something important to say—more important than hypnopaedic slogans—but he doesn't know what it is or how to say it. While the two men share a slight dissonance in their relations with society, they are also uncomfortable with each other's differences.

The workings of society are revealed during Henry and Lenina's date (when they catch an updraft in their plane, and realize it was the cremation of a person), Bernard and Helmholtz's conversation, and Bernard's biweekly Solidarity

Meeting, where he meets with eleven other citizens in an ersatz religious ceremony designed to annihilate individuality in favor of identification with the group. Bernard's failure to achieve rapture during the meeting strengthens his feelings of isolation.

Lenina and Bernard date a few times before the scheduled trip to the Savage Reservation, and Lenina is a bit disturbed by Bernard's oddness. For example, he considers Obstacle Golf a waste of time, preferring to walk and talk—a preference that astonishes Lenina—and he actually says he would prefer to be himself and nasty rather than taking soma and becoming nice and happy. He makes her very uncomfortable when he arranges for the two of them to be alone together, instead of in a large social crowd. Lenina is curious to see the Reservation, though, and Bernard is one of the few who can get a permit to do so.

When Bernard takes his permit to the Director for a signature, the D.H.C. embarrasses him by recalling a trip he had taken there twenty or twenty-five years before, with a Beta-Minus who became lost on the trip and was presumed dead. Then he becomes angry at himself for sharing the story; he warns Bernard that his anti-social behavior and attitudes are unacceptable, and threatens to banish him to a new posting in Iceland.

When Bernard and Lenina go to New Mexico to visit the Savage Reservation, they are warned that an electrified fence surrounds the land and "escape is impossible." Children are still born in this savage place, and those born there are destined to die there. There is little communication with the civilized world; religion, disease, and pests still flourish here. As they prepare to enter the reservation, Bernard calls Helmholtz and learns that the D.H.C. is trying to replace him; he may indeed be sent to Iceland.

From the moment they land on the reservation, Lenina finds cause for complaint—the smells, dust, flies, having to walk, the lack of communal feeling with the natives. She is astounded and disgusted when she catches sight of an old man who has not been chemically preserved, and upset when she reaches for her soma, to help her deal with the unpleasantness, and discovers that neither she nor Bernard has any. Her only pleasure comes when she hears the native drums, beating out the same pulsing rhythms used in "orgyporgy" solidarity meetings to help people achieve rapture.

They watch a religious rite to insure rain and crop growth; it involves whipping a young man until he finally falls to the ground. A short time later they meet John, who is jealous of the man chosen to be whipped; he could have lasted twice as long, he claims, but the people are prejudiced against him because of his skin color. John tells them that his mother, Linda, had come from the Other Place with a man who was his father, "Tomakin." (Bernard excitedly recalls that the D.H.C.'s name is Thomas.) The man had gone away and left Linda there, and John was born on the reservation.

While Lenina spends time with the (to her) disgusting Linda, Bernard questions John about his life on the reservation, and John's answers reveal the difficulties Linda has had, trying to adapt to an alien culture. The women hate her because she believes "every one belongs to every one else"— including their husbands. A culture that promotes consumption to keep employment high, that insists on throwing away clothing rather than mending it, has not taught her how to make the most of limited resources. And despite the fact that she grew up in the "civilized" world, her experiences as a Beta left her without skills or knowledge of anything except the very limited place she was bred to fill. And, worse horror, she had had to face everything without soma, which did not exist on the reservation.

John grows up with fantastic tales of the Other Place, where his parents came from, and the native tales told by the savages. Linda taught him to read, but he has only two books: one of instructions for Beta Embryo-Storage Workers, and the other an ancient volume that one of the savages brings him: *The Complete Works of William Shakespeare*. The magical words weave new half-understood images, which combine with the ones from his mother's world and the reservation in a confusing brew.

Although he is allowed to attend some of the native rituals, John is crushed when the girl he loves marries another, and the boys refuse to allow him to join them in a coming-of-age ceremony. Bernard confides that he, too, feels alone, something John had thought impossible in the Other Place. He asks if John would like to visit the Other Place, thinking he might use his knowledge of who John's father must be to his own advantage. [When John enthusiastically accepts, Bernard contacts Mustapha Mond, who arranges for permits for Linda and John to leave the reservation.]

When Bernard returns from his vacation, the Director tries to humiliate him by accusing him in public of un-Fordlike activities that harm the community. Bernard responds by presenting Linda and John, explaining to the crowd that these are the Director's son and the son's mother. The Director immediately resigns, but everyone else wants to see this creature who had walked up to him and called him "father." (No one cared to see Linda, though, so when she began taking quantities of soma that would soon prove fatal, the doctors did not interfere.)

Bernard's social stature, now that he is John's accredited guardian, has risen greatly; people who shunned him in the past now seek him out, and he delights in the adulation of a society he had previously rejected. His written reports on John reveal that he still has an attachment to his mother, which is considered unnatural, and that he is disturbed by the sets of clones bred to perform specific, repetitive tasks. He is intrigued, though by the Alpha Double Pluses, who are all individuals—one egg, one person. They seem intelligent, but don't do any recreational reading, preferring the feelies (virtual reality movies) instead.

Lenina has also become a celebrity because of her connection with the Savage. He seems to have a crush on her, and she sees no reason why they should not have sex, but he is reticent, even after they attend the feelies together. When John starts refusing to attend Bernard's parties, Bernard's social standing plummets. But John does find Helmholtz congenial, and introduces the young wordsmith to the words of Shakespeare. Initially excited by the masterful use of words, Helmholtz eventually finds the situations in Shakespeare's plays too outlandish for enjoyment. (In *Romeo and Juliet*, for example, he cannot conceive of a girl's parents caring whom she is with.)

Lenina finds herself thinking of no one but John, no matter how many other men she goes out with. John has loved Lenina since they met; he wants to prove himself to her, prove himself worthy of her, so they can be married. Their cultures clash when Lenina visits him and tries to give herself to him; he suddenly uses the words the savages had flung at his mother: whore, strumpet. Their confrontation ends when he gets a phone call, informing him his mother is dying.

He rushes to the hospital and outrages the nurses by insisting on seeing Linda. He is with her when she dies. Leaving her, he finds himself in the middle of a soma distribution in the hospital lobby, and pleads with the assembled Deltas to stop taking soma because it poisons the soul. When they do not respond to his plea, he begins tossing the drug out a window. Bernard, summoned by a friend who sees the Savage making trouble, and Helmholtz rush to the hospital just as the enraged Deltas begin to attack John. Helmholtz and Bernard rush to John's defense, but local police move in and efficiently begin spraying soma in the air.

Once the riot has been quelled, the police take John, Bernard, and Helmholtz to the Controller's office. When Mustapha Mond quotes Shakespeare to John, he is excited; he has never before met anyone who knows the bard. Mond explains that the books are illegal, but that since he makes the laws, he can break them. John asks why the people cannot be exposed to Shakespeare, and Mond tells him they wouldn't understand. Thinking of Helmholtz's response to the tragedy of Romeo and Juliet, he agrees, but suggests they should be given something that would be like Shakespeare, only new so they could understand it. Helmholtz chimes in that this is the kind of thing he would like to write, and the Controller explains that social stability would be upset if people were exposed to tragedy.

As the Controller defends the present system, he notes that even science has to be contained. He mentions that the three miscreants are to be sent to an island, and Bernard breaks down, pleading not to be sent away. Mustapha has him carried from the room; after he is gone, he tells Helmholtz that Bernard is lucky, since he will be with the interesting people who have, like him, been unable to conform in the larger society. The Controller had made his own choice, years ago: "Truth's a menace, science is a public danger"—and he chose to stay on the side of orthodoxy. He offers Helmholtz his choice of islands; the man decides he will write better if he has bad conditions, so he asks to be sent to the Falklands—a choice the Controller approves—then leaves the Savage and the Controller alone as he goes to check on Bernard.

When they are alone, Mustapha reveals to John his secret cache of books, and admits that he believes there probably is a god. The Savage says that surely it is natural to believe in God when you're alone, but Mustapha points out that society is arranged so that people almost never are alone, a truth John gloomily admits. John argues that a belief in God would be a reason for patience, self-denial, and chastity; Mustapha argues that allowing any nobility or heroism would lead to instability and the downfall of civilization. The Savage insists that the society needs "something *with* tears for a change. Nothing costs enough here." The Controller counters that the need for violent emotion, for adrenal stimulation, is well satisfied by compulsory Violent Passion Surrogates, taken monthly—all the passion, none of the inconveniences. When John insists he wants the inconveniences, Mustapha points out that he's claiming the right to be unhappy, unhealthy, hungry, and in pain. John defiantly agrees that's what he wants.]

Later, John meets with Bernard and Helmholtz and tells them the Controller has refused his request to go to the islands with them, insisting on continuing with the experiment: his interaction with society. He decides he will run away anyway, eventually choosing to live in an old lighthouse. He plans to live off the land, and is trying to purify himself for what he sees as his unkind treatment of his mother. When some motorists happen to catch sight of him flagellating himself with a whip of knotted cords, they are fascinated, and inform reporters.

When the journalists begin invading his retreat, sticking microphones in his face and asking ridiculous questions, he receives them with violence that increases with each encounter, so after a while they are lurking in hiding around the lighthouse. When he finds himself thinking once again of Lenina, despite his resolution to think only of how he had mistreated Linda, he grabs his whip and begins beating himself again. The performance is caught on film without his knowledge; once the feelie effects are added, the film is an immediate hit, and swarms of helicopters descend on his hiding place, filled with spectators who want to see "the whipping stunt." Another helicopter approaches and lands, delivering Henry and Lenina. Enraged, John rushes at Lenina with the whip; when she tries to flee, she trips and falls. As the crowd roars its approval, he alternates between whipping himself and whipping Lenina, fallen at his feet. The crowd and he become more frenzied, until finally they leave and he collapses.

When John awakes the next day and remembers what had happened, he kills himself (by hanging, the same way Huxley's brother Trev killed himself).

CHRONOLOGY

(Note: Dates given for Huxley's books are for year of first publication; those published during World War II, 1942–1946, were published first in the United States; the rest were published first in England.)

1894

Aldous Huxley is born in the village of Godalming, Surrey, England, July 26.

1898

The United States wins the Spanish-American War (April–August; the treaty officially ending the war is signed in Paris, France, in December), gaining Guam, Puerto Rico, and the Philippines.

1899

The first international discussion of the problems of armaments and warfare is held at The Hague, the Netherlands, May–July, at the invitation of Czar Nicholas II of Russia; delegates from twenty-six nations (including the United States) discuss such issues as disarmament and the establishment of an international tribunal to arbitrate disputes between nations.

1907

The Second International Peace Conference is called by Czar Nicholas II of Russia. (The conference had originally been proposed the previous year by U.S. President Theodore Roosevelt, but was postponed because of the Russo-Japanese War.) As with the first conference (in 1899), little progress is made.

1908

Huxley enters Eton College in September, planning to specialize in biology. In November, his mother, Julia Huxley, dies.

1910

Huxley withdraws from Eton after an attack of *keratitis punctata* causes blindness.

1911

After surgery, Huxley recovers partial sight, but will be plagued with bad eyesight for the rest of his life.

1912

The British liner *Titanic* sinks on its maiden voyage, April 14–15. U.S. troops occupy Tientsin, China, to protect American interests in the Chinese Revolution (which began in October 1911).

1913

Huxley enters Balliol College, Oxford.

1914

Huxley's brother Trevenen commits suicide. Archduke Francis Ferdinand of Austria is assassinated at Sarajevo, Serbia, leading to Austria's declaration of war on Serbia on July 28. Germany declares war on Russia August 1, on France August 3, and on Belgium August 4. On August 4 England declares war on Germany, while the United States declares its neutrality. On August 6, Austria declares war on Russia.

1915

Huxley visits Garsington, home of Philip and Lady Ottoline Morrell; first meets D.H. Lawrence here. The *Lusitania,* a British steamship, is sunk without warning by a German submarine, contributing to the U.S. decision to declare war on Germany two years later.

1916

Huxley receives a First in English Literature at Balliol College, Oxford. Publishes *The Burning Wheel.*

1917

Huxley publishes *Jonah.* Accepts a teaching post at Eton from September 1917 to February 1919. The United States enters World War I in April.

1918

Huxley publishes *The Defeat of Youth, and Other Poems.* World War I ends November 11.

1919

Huxley joins the editorial staff of the *Athenaeum.* Marries Maria Nys, July 10.

1920

Huxley publishes *Limbo* and *Leda.* The Huxleys' son, Matthew, is born in April.

1921

Publishes *Crome Yellow.*

1922

Publishes *Mortal Coils.*

1923

Publishes *On the Margin: Notes and Essays* and *Antic Hay.* Moves to Italy.

1924

Publishes *Little Mexican and Other Stories* (U.S. title: *Young Archimedes, and Other Stories*) and *The Discovery.*

1925

Publishes *Those Barren Leaves, Along the Road: Notes and Essays of a Tourist,* and *Selected Poems.* In September, begins around-the-world trek.

1926

Develops a friendship with D.H. Lawrence. Publishes *Two or Three Graces, and Other Stories, Jesting Pilate,* and *Essays New and Old* (U.S. title: *Essays Old and New*).

1927

Publishes *Proper Studies.* Charles Lindbergh completes the first solo airplane flight across the Atlantic Ocean.

1928

Huxley publishes *Point Counter Point.* Moves to France.

1929

Publishes *Arabia Infelix, and Other Poems, Do What You Will,* and *Holy Face, and Other Essays.* The Great Depression begins in the United States with the stock market crash of October 29.

1930

Huxley publishes *Appenine, Brief Candles,* and *Vulgarity in Literature: Digressions from a Theme.* Visits D.H. Lawrence in France and is with him when Lawrence dies, March 2.

1931

Publishes *Music at Night, and Other Essays, The Cicadas, and Other Poems,* and *The World of Light: A Comedy in Three Acts,* which is produced at the Royalty Theatre in London.

1932

Publishes *Brave New World, Rotunda: A Selection from the Works of Aldous Huxley, Texts and Pretexts: An Anthology with Commentaries,* and *T.H. Huxley as a Man of Letters,* as well as editing *The Letters of D.H. Lawrence.*

1933

Publishes *Retrospect: An Omnibus of Aldous Huxley's Books.*
His father, Leonard Huxley, dies. In the United States, the Humanist Manifesto, signed by several prominent professors, takes a strong stand against capitalism, seeks to erase distinctions between secular and sacred, and declares man the product of evolution, not divine creation.

1934

Publishes *Behind the Mexique Bay* and *Eyeless in Gaza.*

1935

Becomes active in the pacifist movement. After years of debate, the Senate refuses to ratify U.S. membership in the World Court, part of the League of Nations established in 1919.

1936

Publishes *1936 . . . Peace?, The Olive Tree, and Other Essays,* and *What Are You Going to Do About It? The Case for Constructive Pacifism.*

1937

Publishes *Ends and Means: An Enquiry into the Nature of Ideals and into the Methods Employed for Their Realization* and edits *An Encyclopedia of Pacifism.* Travels to the United States. The horrific explosion of the dirigible *Hindenburg* marks the virtual end of lighter-than-air transport.

1938

Huxley moves to Los Angeles, California. Publishes *The Most Agreeable Vice.* Begins writing for the movies.

1939

Huxley publishes *After Many a Summer Dies the Swan* (also called *After Many a Summer*). Germany begins annexing smaller European countries; in August it signs a non-aggression pact with Russia, and on September 1 invades Poland. On September 3, Great Britain and France declare war on Germany; World War II has begun. The United States declares neutrality.

1940

Huxley publishes *Words and Their Meanings.* Germany launches the Battle of Britain in August, intended to destroy the Royal Air Force in preparation for the invasion of England. Germany defeats France, invades Norway, and overruns Denmark, Luxembourg, Belgium, and the Netherlands.

1941

Huxley publishes *Grey Eminence: A Study in Religion and Politics.* Germany invades the U.S.S.R. on June 22. On December

7, Japan bombs the U.S. base at Pearl Harbor, Hawaii. On December 8, Congress declares war on Japan; on December 11 Germany and Italy declare war against the United States.

1942

Huxley publishes *The Art of Seeing.* U.S. forces face many defeats in battles in the Pacific, with a few notable exceptions, including wins against the Japanese in the Battle of the Coral Sea (May) and the Battle of Midway (June).

1944

Huxley publishes *Time Must Have a Stop* and *Twice Seven: Fourteen Selected Stories.* U.S. forces make progress in the Pacific and wreak destruction in North Africa, Italy, and France. Italy falls in May; Allied forces land on France's Normandy beach on D-Day, June 6.

1945

Huxley publishes *The Perennial Philosophy.* Germany surrenders May 7. The United States drops the world's first atomic bombs on the Japanese cities of Hiroshima (August 6) and Nagasaki (August 9); the Japanese surrender August 14.

1946

Huxley publishes *Verses and a Comedy* and *Science, Liberty and Peace.*

1948

Publishes *The Gioconda Smile: A Play.*

1949

Publishes *Ape and Essence.*

1950

Huxley publishes *Themes and Variations.* U.S. President Harry Truman authorizes development of the hydrogen bomb. North Korea invades South Korea, beginning the Korean War (1950–53); U.S. forces are sent to help defend South Korea under the aegis of the United Nations.

1951

When Chinese troops enter the Korean War, a third world war is averted when the United Nations decides not to attack Chinese bases, and the United States agrees. World War II is finally formally over: A peace treaty with Japan is signed by 48 nations, and the state of war with Germany is declared officially ended by President Harry Truman.

1952

Publishes *The Devils of Loudun.*

1953

Takes the hallucinogenic drug mescaline under the supervision of Dr. Humphrey Osmand. Over the next decade, he will take hallucinogenic drugs nine to twelve times. The Korean War ends. Julius and Ethel Rosenberg are executed June 19, the first civilians to be executed in the United States for espionage.

1954

Huxley publishes *The Doors of Perception.*

1955

Huxley's wife, Maria, dies in February. Publishes *The Genius and the Goddess.*

1956

Marries Laura Archera, March 19. Publishes *Heaven and Hell* and *Adonis and the Alphabet, and Other Essays* (U.S. title: *Tomorrow and Tomorrow and Tomorrow, and Other Essays*).

1957

Publishes *Collected Short Stories.* Russia launches *Sputnik I,* the first artificial Earth satellite.

1958

Huxley publishes *Brave New World Revisited.*

1959

Publishes *Collected Essays.* Lectures on "The Human Situation" as visiting professor at the University of California at Santa Barbara. Receives the Award of Merit for the Novel from the American Academy of Arts and Letters.

1960

Publishes *On Art and Artists* (edited by Morris Philipson). Presents a series of lectures, "What a Piece of Work Is Man," as Centennial Carnegie Visiting Professor at the Massachusetts Institute of Technology. Is diagnosed as having cancer of the tongue.

1961

The Huxley home in Los Angeles is destroyed by fire. President John F. Kennedy urges U.S. families to buy or build fallout shelters in case of atomic war.

1962

Publishes *Island* while serving a stint as visiting professor at the University of California, Berkeley. Elected a Companion of Literature by England's Royal Society of Literature. The United States blockades Cuba after finding evidence of Soviet-built missile bases on the island, just 90 miles from the

American mainland. Russian Premier Khrushchev agrees to remove the bases under UN supervision.

1963

Huxley publishes *Literature and Science.* Dies of cancer in Los Angeles on November 22, a few hours later and on the same day U.S. President John F. Kennedy is assassinated.

1969

Letters of Aldous Huxley published (edited by Grover Smith).

1977

The Human Situation: Lectures at Santa Barbara, 1959 published (edited by Piero Ferrucci).

FOR FURTHER RESEARCH

John Atkins, *Aldous Huxley: A Literary Study.* Revised edition. New York: Orion, 1967.

Sybille Bedford, *Aldous Huxley: A Biography.* New York: Alfred A. Knopf/Harper & Row, 1974.

Milton Birnbaum, *Aldous Huxley's Search for Values.* Knoxville: University of Tennessee Press, 1971.

Laurence Brander, *Aldous Huxley: A Critical Study.* Lewisburg, PA: Bucknell University Press; Cranbury, NJ: Associated University Presses, 1970.

Jenni Calder, *Huxley and Orwell:* Brave New World *and* Nineteen Eighty-Four. London: Edward Arnold, 1976.

B.L. Chakoo, *Aldous Huxley and Eastern Wisdom.* Atlantic Highlands, NJ: Humanities Press, 1981.

Virginia M. Clark, *Aldous Huxley and Film.* Metuchen, NJ: Scarecrow Press, 1987.

David King Dunaway, *Huxley in Hollywood.* London: Bloomsbury, 1989.

Claire John Eschelbach and Joyce Lee Shober, *Aldous Huxley: A Bibliography, 1916–1959.* Berkeley: University of California Press, 1961.

C.S. Ferns, *Aldous Huxley: Novelist.* London: Athlone Press, 1980.

Peter Firchow, *Aldous Huxley: Satirist and Novelist.* Minneapolis: University of Minnesota Press, 1972.

Peter Edgerly Firchow, *The End of Utopia: A Study of Aldous Huxley's* Brave New World. Lewisburg, PA: Bucknell University Press; Cranbury, NJ: Associated University Presses, 1984.

Sisirkumar Ghose, *Aldous Huxley: A Cynical Salvationist.* London: Asia Publishing House, 1962.

Alexander Henderson, *Aldous Huxley.* New York: Russell & Russell, 1964.

Charles M. Holmes, *Aldous Huxley and the Way to Reality.* Bloomington: Indiana University Press, 1970.

Julian Huxley, ed., *Aldous Huxley, 1894–1963: A Memorial Volume.* New York: Harper & Row, 1965.

Laura Archera Huxley, *This Timeless Moment: A Personal View of Aldous Huxley.* New York: Farrar, Straus & Giroux, 1968.

Dattatreya Vishnu Jog, *Aldous Huxley the Novelist.* Bombay, India: The Book Centre, n.d.

Robert E. Kuehn, ed., *Aldous Huxley: A Collection of Critical Essays.* Englewood Cliffs, NJ: Prentice-Hall, 1974.

Keith May, *Aldous Huxley.* New York: Barnes & Noble, 1972.

Jerome Meckier, *Aldous Huxley: Satire and Structure.* New York: Barnes & Noble, 1969.

Guinevera A. Nance, *Aldous Huxley.* New York: Continuum, 1988.

Philip Thody, *Huxley: A Biographical Introduction.* New York: Scribner's, 1973.

EDITIONS OF *BRAVE NEW WORLD*

Brave New World, abridged and simplified by H.A. Cartledge. London: Longman, 1973.

Brave New World and *Brave New World Revisited,* with a foreword by the author; introduction by Martin Green. New York: Harper & Row, 1965.

Brave New World with the author's foreword; introduction by Ashley Montagu; illus. by Mara McAfee. Norwalk, CT: Easton Press, 1978.

THE WORLD WIDE WEB

At this writing, there does not seem to be an "official" Aldous Huxley site, nor a major site affiliated with a university. However, searches on a variety of search engines produce thousands of links to sites that at least mention Huxley's name in connection with anything to archeology to hallucinogenic drug use. These two sites offer a variety of links to more information, especially about his literary works:

http://www.primenet.com/~matthew/huxley/

http://www.levity.com/corduroy/huxley.htm

INDEX